MacBook Air (2020 Model) For Seniors

GETTING STARTED WITH YOUR FIRST MAC

Scott La Counte

RIDICULOUSLY
SIMPLE BOOKS

ANAHEIM, CALIFORNIA

www.RidiculouslySimpleBooks.com

Copyright © 2020 by Scott La Counte.

Table of Contents

Introduction *12*

Let's Talk Mac *13*

  Fewer Viruses 13

  Keeping It Simple 14

  No Bloat 15

  A Look At the Hardware 15

  MacBook Pro vs. MacBook Air 16

Mac For the Windows User *17*

  Right Click 17

  Keyboard Shortcuts...18

  Transferring Documents 19

  Compatibility...20

  Setup Assistant 21

What's Catalina OS All About? *23*

The Mac Crash Course *25*

  Keyboard..25

  Force Touch 26

  The Desktop...28

  Apple Has a Dark Secret 28

  It's Dynamic!..30

  This OS is Stacked 30

  Menu Bar 32

  Menulets 32

  Dock...32

Trash 33

App Buttons 34

Launchpad 34

Notifications 36

Split View 37

Tabbed Software 40

Picture-In-Picture Video 41

Using Notes 42

    The Notes Crash Course 42

    Views 43

    Folders 43

    Viewing Attachments 45

    Delete Note 46

    Creating a Note 46

    Lock Note 46

    Create a Table 47

    Create a Checklist 48

    Add a Style 49

    Adding Sketches and Images 50

    Adding Collaborators 52

    Sharing Notes 53

    Searching Notes 54

    Exporting Notes 54

    Pinning Notes 55

    Attaching Files 56

    Spell Check 56

    Font Formatter 57

How To Find Things 58

Finder 58

Finder Reimagined 59

Other Views 60

Sorting in Finder 62

File Management 63

Favorites 64

Tabbed Browsing 65

Tags 66

Surfing the Internet On Mac 67

Setting Up With Ethernet 67

Setting Up Wireless Networks 68

Airport Express / Airport Extreme 69

Safari 69

The Toolbar 71

All About Tabs 74

Private Window... 75

A History of You 76

Bookmarks / Reading List 78

Exporting 80

Reader Mode.. 80

Emoji That 82

Find It 83

What's Up Dock?... 84

Default Browser... 84

Importing Bookmarks 85

Safari for Windows 86

Safari Extensions 87

Find Extensions.. 87

Add an Extension 87

Using Extensions 89

Uninstalling Extensions.. 89

Privacy and Security 90

General... 90

Tabs 91

AutoFill.. 91

Passwords 92

Search.. 92

Security.. 92

Privacy 93

Websites 93

Extensions... 93

Advanced 94

Safari Preferences.. 94

Creating Strong Passwords 95

Firewall 96

Find My Mac 96

Privacy 97

Internet Privacy.. 97

Application Privacy 98
Screen Time...98

Mail **101**

Adding Accounts **101**

Sending an Email **102**

There's An App For That...*104*

Phone Calls **105**

Contacts **105**

iMessage **106**

FaceTime **108**

Photo Booth **109**

Calendar **113**

Reminders **115**

Mail **116**
Mail Crash Course...117

Location Based Reminder **119**

Notes **120**

Creating and Editing Notes...................................... **121**

iTunes In a Non-iTunes World **122**
Show the iTunes Store in Apple Music.................................122

App Store **125**

Photos.. **128**

Lesser Used Apps **133**

Siri **134**

MacOS Meet iOS **135**

Apple Services *137*

Introduction **137**

iCloud **138**
Where Is iCloud?...139
Backing Up Your Computer With iCloud 140
iCloud Drive 140

Apple Arcade 141

How to Sign Up 141

Cancelling Arcade Subscription 142

Apple TV+ 143

Apple Music 145

Apple Music Crash Course 145

Library 146

For You 146

Browse 147

Radio 147

Search 148

Listening to Music and Creating a Playlist 148

Tips for Getting the Most Out of Apple Music 151

Apple News 152

Apple News Crash Course 153

Today 153

News+ 156

Apple Card 158

Getting Your Card 159

When There Is No Apple Pay 160

Seeing Card Activity 164

Making Payments and Seeing Statements 167

System Settings 170

System Preferences 170

Sound 177

Users & Groups 178

Snap This 181

Continue That Photo Where You Left Off 182

Accessibility 183

Voice Control 185

Sidecar 186

Privacy and Security 189

Screen Time 192

Keep It running Smoothly 196

Preserving Battery Life 196

iCloud 197

Time Machine 198

Software Updates 199

iWork for Mac *200*

How To Get Pages 200

Running Pages for the First Time 202

The Pages Crash Course 202
  Select 204
  Select Paragraph 204
  Select All 205
  Select Options 205
  Cut, Copy and Paste 205
  Find and Replace 205
  Define 206
  Copy Style 207
  Inserting Hyperlinks 208
  Undo/Redo 208
  Hands-On Exercise 209

The Formatting Toolbar 209
  Hands-On Exercise 212

Layout 213

More 213

Opening Pages From iCloud 214

Managing Documents 215
  Renaming Documents 215

Hands-On Exercise 216

Inserting An Image 217

Arranging Images 218
  Resize and Rotate 219
  Text Wrap and Placement 220
  Image Grouping 224
  Watermarks 225

Edit Mask and Alpha 226

Styling Your Image 229
  Basic Styles 229

Border..230

Shadow..231

Reflection..233

Transparency..233

Hands-on Exercise..**234**

Inserting a Table...**235**

Adding Columns and Rows...235

Interacting with Tables..**236**

Row / Column Options..**237**

Styling Tables..**237**

Table Options 237

Cell Options 238

Text Options 240

Arrange Options 242

Deleting Tables...**242**

Importing Tables...**242**

Hands-on Exercise..**243**

Inserting a Chart..**244**

Editing Chart Data..**245**

Styling Your Pie Chart..**246**

Styling Your Bar Chart..**252**

Hands-On Exercise...**253**

Inserting a Shape...**254**

Resizing Shapes and Adjusting Proportions....................**255**

Moving and Rotating Shapes 256

Adding Text to a Shape 256

Creating Text Boxes...**257**

Styling Shapes and Text Boxes **259**

Hands-On Exercise **259**

Entering Document Setup Mode **261**

Changing Document Margins and Size **262**

Creating Custom Paper Size..**263**

Hyphenations and Ligatures 264

Headers and Page Numbers 265

Bookmarks 266

Table of Contents 267

Insert Footnotes 269

Insert Comment 269

Track Changes 270

Syncing Documents with iCloud 271

Emailing a Document From Pages 271

Collaborating 271

Export a Pages Document 272

Printing 273

Appendix: Keyboard Shortcuts 275

General Shortcuts 275

Document Shortcuts 276

About the Author 277

Disclaimer: Please note, while every effort has been made to ensure accuracy, this book is not endorsed by Apple, Inc. and should be considered unofficial.

INTRODUCTION

You know what a MacBook is, but chances are you spent most of your life with a Windows PC.

While there is a learning curve, it's not as hard as you'd think. And there are lots of advantages—especially if you have other Apple products like the iPhone, Apple Watch, iPad, and Apple TV.

This book is meant to help users who are picking up a MacBook for the first time. While it's based off the MacBook Air (2020 model), you will be fine if you own any other current Mac model.

The following topics will be covered inside:

- What's the difference between all the different Macs and MacBook's
- Accessibility features
- How do you do all those Windows "things" on a Mac
- Using the Magic Mouse and Force Touch
- Using Siri
- Using Safari to search the Internet
- How to find things / how to organize things to make them easy to find
- Using Sidecar
- Using Notes
- Using iWorks
- Downloading / Updating apps on the App Store
- Organizing photos
- Making phone calls and sending messages
- Multitasking
- And much, much more!

[1]

LET'S TALK MAC

> This chapter will cover:
> - What's so great about Macs
> - Are they really virus free?
> - OS without the bloat
> - A look at the hardware

Before diving into the actual software, let's address the obvious: why pick Mac?

I was in the Windows camp for a long time; I'd see the Mac and think it was just a computer for hipsters. Sure they were nice to look at—they were shiny and didn't look plastic-y and cheap…but they were also expensive.

But then I actually used one, and I was blown away. Here's why…

FEWER VIRUSES

You've probably heard someone say they use a Mac because they don't get viruses. That's not true. Any computer can get a virus. But it

is true that Macs are generally less prone to viruses and are more secure.

The reason you don't hear about Mac viruses very often is twofold:

1. While it's hard to pinpoint just how many computers there
   are in the world, most computers are still Windows. So, if you
   are a hacker wanting to wreak havoc into cyberspace, then
   your obvious target would be the one with the largest audi-
   ence.

2. The second reason is MacOS is built by Apple, for Apple.
   Windows builds their OS to be built for essentially any computer, which opens the door for vulnerabilities.

I know a lot of Mac users and rarely do I hear someone say they
have a virus. If you are concerned, however, one popular free virus pro-
tector is called Bitdefender Virus Scanner (http://www.bitde-
fender.com/).

KEEPING IT SIMPLE

When it comes to design, Apple likes to make things that are beautiful and simple. This philosophy can be seen in their watches, iPhones,
and iPads—across all their products.

Because Apple spends so much time keeping it simple, you also
have seen the last days of computer crashes and blue screens of
deaths.

Apple spends a lot of time thinking not just about what the computer should do, but how people will do it. If you've been using Windows all of your life, then all the different menus and buttons might
seem intimidating at first—but don't stress! This book will show you
how much easier it actually is.

If you have any other Apple products, then many of the common
Mac tasks will probably seem very similar to you. What's more, if you
have an iPhone, iPad, or even Apple TV, then they all work and interact
with each other.

No Bloat

I remember my last Windows computer. I couldn't wait to turn it on…and then I couldn't wait to turn it off! Your first hour should be spent just having fun exploring it, but my first hour was spent uninstalling programs!

One reason Windows computers are cheaper is that manufacturers team up with software companies and install all kinds of unnecessary programs—most of them are just free trials.

With Mac, you turn your computer on for the first time, create an ID if you don't already have one, put in your Wi-Fi, and log in to iTunes / iCloud. That's it. It should take less than ten minutes to get your computer up and running once you get it out of the box.

A Look At the Hardware

In 2008, the MacBook Air was revolutionary. It was powerful, and yet thin enough to fit in an envelope! Years past, and it became a little less revolutionary. Other computers were just as thin, but even more powerful.

The 2020 model, however, put MacBook Air back in the spotlight with a new model that had a Retina display (older models did not), fingerprint sensor, and power that was almost equal to MacBook Pros.

There aren't a lot of ports on MacBook Air's. One side is two Thunderbolt 3 / USB-c ports (this is where your power will plug in as well); USB-c is the new standard of USB and lets you transfer data at a much faster rate. If you still need regular adapters you can buy them cheap; you can also buy USB drives with both USB and USB-c connections.

The reverse side has a headphone jack; MacBook Airs have Bluetooth, so you can also listen to music with a wireless headphone—or you can use the computers built-in speakers.

MacBook Pro vs. MacBook Air

MacBook Air's used to be the lightest notebook in Apple's lineup; they still are. But MacBook Pros are only slightly heavier. So, weight is no longer the deciding factor for most people.

What's right for you?

Air's come in one screen size; if you want a larger screen, then Pro's are your only option.

The processors on the Pro and Air are comparable, but the Pro is slightly faster; the Pro also can be configured higher—meaning you can upgrade it to higher standards. The Pro's also have the edge on graphic cards, but the Airs still have very good cards. Airs can only be upgraded to 16GB of RAM; the 15 inch Pro (not the 13 inch) can be up-graded to 32GB

Battery-wise, the Airs get 12 hours vs the 10 hours on a Pro.

Pro's are currently the only notebooks that have the Touch Bar on the keyboard.

Finally, Pros have two additional USB-c ports.

[2]

MAC FOR THE WINDOWS USER

This chapter will cover:
- How to use Windows OS features on MacOS
- Transferring docs
- Compatibility
- Setup Assistant

So exactly how is Mac different from Windows? Throughout the book, I'll be making comparisons to help you, but first I want to give a rundown of some of the major differences.

RIGHT CLICK

Right-clicking is probably second nature to you if you are a Windows user; on the Mac, it's all about gestures—touching the Trackpad (Mac's mouse) a certain way (or on new Macs, using more or less pressure) will bring up different options and menus.

As weird as it sounds, the first time I used a Mac, the right-click (or lack thereof) drove me crazy...until I figured out that right-clicking was actually there. To right-click on a Mac, click with two fingers instead of one. Alternatively, you can press Control and click with one finger.

If you have an old Windows USB mouse, you don't have to toss it—you can plug it into your Mac and it will work with no installation. The right-click will even work.

I'll explain how to customize your Trackpad later in the book, but if you'd like to jump ahead, you can go to System Preferences > Track-pad.

And don't worry about messing something up; it's very hard to harm a Mac!

KEYBOARD SHORTCUTS

This section will give you a very quick rundown of the more popular keyboard shortcuts; for a more detailed list, see Appendix A at the end of this book.

On a Windows computer, you might be used to using Control (CTRL) frequently; Control is on the Mac keyboard, but don't get con-fused—on a Mac, the Control button equivalent is the Command (⌘) Key (to the right of the keyboard). The good news is the letter combi-nation for the most frequently used Windows shortcuts is almost al-ways the same on a Mac—Control-C to copy is Command-C on the Mac; Control-X to Cut is Command-X; Control-V to Paste is Command-V.

On a Windows computer, you can hold Alt and Tab to cycle through programs...on a Mac you use Command and Tab.

The two most frequently used function keys (the buttons above the numbers) are F3 and F4; F3 will show a list of the programs you have open, and F4 brings up your Launchpad (all of your available pro-grams...kind of like the Start menu on Windows).

Just keep reminding yourself that while it looks different, it's really not...Windows has File Explorer, Mac has Finder; Windows has the Start Menu, Mac has Launchpad; Windows has the Ribbon menu, Mac has the Top Navigation menu.

Below is a quick overview of what things are called on Windows and what they are called on a Mac:

Windows	Mac
Windows Explorer / My Computer / Computer	Finder
Control Panel	System Preferences
Programs	Applications (often shortened to apps)
Task Bar and Start Menu	Dock
Tray	Menulets
Recycle Bin	Trash
Task Manager	Activity Monitor
Media Center	iTunes

TRANSFERRING DOCUMENTS

The thing a lot of people worry about when updating any computer is how to get all of your information from your old computer to your new computer. With Macs, it's a pretty simple task—you can even take it into your local Apple Store for free help (appointments are needed, so don't just walk in).

If you don't want to wait for an appointment or you just like doing things on your own, there's already a tool on your computer to help: it's called Migration Assistant. Be advised, you do need an Internet connection.

To start, go to your Windows computer and either search any search engine for "Windows Migration Assistant" or go directly to https://support.apple.com/kb/DL1557?locale=en_US. Once you are there, download and install the program on your Windows computer.

Windows Migration Assistant v1.0.5.7

Download

This software will help you migrate data from a Windows PC running Windows XP, Windows Vista, Windows 7 or Windows 8. The Migration Assistant will launch automatically after it has been installed.

For more information, please see http://support.apple.com/kb/HT4796.

From your Mac, click the Launchpad icon (i.e. the rocket on your taskbar).

Next, click on Other and then click Migration Assistant.

To use Migration Assistant, everything that is open on your Mac will be closed, so make sure and save your work, and don't start until you are ready.

From the setup, click Continue, and then select "From another Mac, PC, Time Machine backup, or other disk," then select Continue and then "From another Mac or PC." The next window should show the Windows computer that you want to transfer files from. Click Continue, verify on the Windows computer that the passcodes match and click Continue again. Lastly, the assistant will ask you to select the types of files you want to transfer.

If you don't do the assistant right away, you can always use it later. There's no timeline for using it, so if you dig up an older Windows computer in the garage and want to transfer everything from it, the option will always be there.

COMPATIBILITY

Now that you have everything copied over, let's talk briefly about compatibility. While many files will open on a Mac, the software will not. That means if you have Word on Windows, you can't just move it over; most popular software (like Word) is available on the Mac, but you will have to purchase it.

Don't stress too much; most the files that you have just transferred will actually still open even if you don't buy software to open them. Word files (Doc, Docx) for example, will open in Pages (which is free on new Macs).

If your file does not open, then you will probably be able to find free software online that will open it.

SETUP ASSISTANT

If you are starting up the Mac for the first time (and you are the first owner), then the first thing that will happen is an automated setup assistant will guide you through creating an account and getting everything set up.

The first thing you'll do is select your country; if you don't see yours, then click See All. Click Continue after you finish each section. Next, you'll choose your keyboard layout; if you are an English speaker, then the United States is probably your first bet, but if you are going to be typing primarily in another language (like Chinese) then you may want to pick that country instead—this can be changed later.

Picking the wireless network is the next thing you will see after clicking Continue—you don't have to set up wireless at this point, but if you do, it will also trigger the Migration Assistant (which will help you transfer files); this is all optional so you can skip it (you can also come back to it later).

The next screen is one of the most important: entering your Apple ID. If you have any other Apple devices (iPad, iPod, iPhone, etc.) or if you have an ID that you use with Windows, then you'll want to use it because all of the apps, music and other media you've paid for are tied to your account. If you don't have one, you'll have the option of getting one—it's free and includes iCloud (also free), which I'll be talking about later.

The next part of the setup is Find My Mac (which you need iCloud for); this is a great feature that lets you see where your Mac is from your Internet browser; if it's been stolen it also lets you wipe away all of your content.

After agreeing to the terms, you'll be taken to the Time Zone selection. After that, you are asked if you want to enable the iCloud Keychain. What's the iCloud Keychain? Basically, this stores passwords in the Cloud so you can use them on any device.

Next, decide if you want to send diagnostics and usage data to Apple; this is all for statistical purposes to help Apple make their software and hardware better, but it's entirely up to you. It won't slow your computer down if you do decide to do it—it's all done in the background. After this step, you decide if you want to register your installation with Apple.

Finally, you are ready to start using your Mac!

[3]

WHAT'S CATALINA OS ALL ABOUT?

This chapter will cover:
- What's new in the latest update?

How do you perfect something that most people are pretty happy with? With tweaks that are small that make things smarter, and more intuitive—sometimes without you even noticing. Some might say that MacOS has less new than any other Apple hardware. That means the learning curve for older users will be a breeze. But there's still a lot of smaller things that can help you be even more efficient on your Mac.

- **iTunes** - Perhaps the biggest feature is not an improvement but an elimination. iTunes is gone! Gone, but not forgotten, many of Apple's features still exist in other apps. Instead of going to iTunes to purchase your content, you now go to dedicated apps: Apple Music (for music), Apple TV (for TV and Movies), Apple Books (for books), and the App Store (for Mac Apps).
- **Device Management** - Prior to Catalina, you could manage your devices in iTunes; with iTunes gone, this action can be performed in Finder.
- **Sidecar** - Let's you use your iPad as a second screen.

- **Screen Time** - The popular iPhone and iPad app that lets you track and manage the amount of time you spend on your device is now on Mac.
- **Photos** - UI (user interface) improvements.
- **Apple Arcade** - Apple's newest service is available on iPhone, Apple TV, iPad, and now MacOS.
- **Security** - New protocol is in place to make sure your Mac is secure; you won't see an app for this, but it's running in the background.
- **Mail** - New blocking feature.
- **Reminders** - New user interface that's more aligned with what you see on iPhones and iPads.
- **Notes** - New gallery view to make it easier to visually see your notes.
- **Voice control** - Accessibility feature that lets you run your computer with your voice.

[3]

THE MAC CRASH COURSE

This chapter will cover:
- Magic Mouse and ForceTouch
- The desktop
- Dark mode
- Dynamic mode
- Stacked icons
- Menu
- The Dock
- Split View
- Tabbed software
- Picture-in-picture video

The best way to learn is by doing, so I'm sure you're eager to get your hands wet and start using the Mac! If you are new to Mac, however, that can be a little intimating—it's not hard to use, but you have to, at the very least, know what you are looking at. In this chapter, I'll give you a crash course in the MacOS interface. By the end of the chapter, you won't be an expert, but you'll know where things are and how to start opening and using things.

KEYBOARD

The keyboard?! I know what you're thinking: a keyboard is a keyboard! Well, sort of. While it is true that you could use a Windows keyboard on a Mac, there are keyboards (including the one that's free with your Mac or built into your MacBook) that are specifically designed for Mac.

There are not a lot of differences; below are the four main ones.

Apple Key

On a Windows keyboard, there is a button that looks like a Windows flag called the Windows Button. There's no sense putting a Windows button on a Mac keyboard, so where the Windows button normally is, you'll find the Apple button, which doesn't look at all like an apple! It actually looks like this (⌘); it's more commonly known as the Command Button—though some people also call it the Clover Key and Pretzel Key.

Delete (Backspace)

On a Windows keyboard, the backspace button is a 'Backwards Delete' key and the delete button is a 'Forward Delete' key (removing the space immediately after the cursor). On a Mac keyboard, the backspace key is labeled 'Delete' and is in exactly the same location as the Windows backspace key. Most Mac keyboards don't have a Forward Delete key anymore, though larger ones do—it's called "Del->". If you don't see it, you still can use forward delete by hitting the FN button (button left corner of your keyboard) and Delete button.

FORCE TOUCH

If you have the latest MacBook Air then you will have a brand new feature called Force Touch; Force Touch is something you'll soon see on all iPhones, iPads and pretty much every new Apple device—it's actually already on the Apple Watch. So what is it? It measures how much pressure you are giving the Trackpad—if you tap down on your Trackpad over an icon or image, and then press all the way, it will show you a preview of it.

On iPhones this feature is called "3D Touch"; it's a little different, but it's basically the same.

You can change your Force Touch settings by going into System Preference and Mouse / Trackpad.

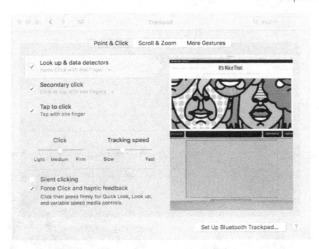

You'll notice when you push down on your Trackpad, it feels like it's clicking twice; when your computer is off, it won't feel like that because you need the computer powered on for the force feedback to work.

Here's a brief overview of some of the things you can do with Force Touch; as you use your Mac, you'll discover dozens and dozens more—especially as developers begin to implement it in software.

- Look up – Force click the text in a webpage and a popover appears, showing you Lookup results for that text. It may be a dictionary, Wikipedia page or something else.
- Addresses – Force click an address to see a Maps preview of that location.
- Events – Force click dates and events to add them to Calendar.
- Link previews – Force click a link in Safari or Mail to see an inline preview of the webpage.
- File icons – Force click a file icon to see a Quick Look preview of the file's content.
- File names – Force click a file name in the Finder or on your desktop to edit the file name.
- Dock – Force click an app icon in the Dock to access App Exposé. This shows you all open windows for that app.
- QuickTime and iMovie – You can vary the pressure you use on fast-forward and rewind buttons.
- Map zooming – Press harder on a zoom button to accelerate as you zoom in and out of a map.

The Desktop

Hopefully, by now, your files are transferred, you've completed the initial startup, and you have a pretty picture on your desktop. At last, you are ready to use your computer!

The desktop is where you'll be spending much of your time, so let's take some time getting to know it.

The first thing you should notice is that it's really not that much different from Windows—it's a vast space that you can either leave empty or fill with icons or documents.

Apple Has a Dark Secret

Deep in the halls of Apple, developers have been working on something very...dark. It's called Dark Mode. Does anyone want to guess what happens when you switch it on? If you said "Disney emoji's dance happily on your screen" then go back and reread the question. So, what is dark mode and why would you want to use it?

The point of dark mode is to put an emphasis on what you are working on or what you need to find. Let's say you're editing a photo. What's important? The photo. All those things in the background are just noise. Sometimes you need the noise for what you're working on, but you'll work more effectively by having them darkened. It's not like things in the background are harder to see—the contrast just helps you be more creative. At least that's what Apple thinks. If you think otherwise, you have the option to turn it off.

In the image above, you can see the difference between dark mode (left) and light mode (right). In dark mode, those thumbnails should pop a little more than in light mode.

Not all apps will look different. It's up to the company that makes the app to redesign an app that takes advantage of it. Apple has obviously updated many of its apps (like Calendar, iTunes, Mail).

If you've updated to MacOS Catalina then you'll be asked if you want it on. If you want to turn it on, or if you turned it off but now want it on, it's easy to do:

Go to System Preferences (you'll find that in the app launch area of your Dock).

Select General and select the option.

When you're in System Preferences > General, you'll also notice you have the option to change the accent color that goes along with light / dark mode; this changes all the arrows, toggles, etc. throughout the OS. You can always go back to default settings, so don't be afraid to play around: you won't break anything!

IT'S DYNAMIC!

Apple always likes to put emphasis on making things more aesthetically pleasing when they update the OS. Dark mode is one way they do that; Dynamic Desktop is another.

When I heard the name, I imagined it would let your wallpaper come alive by having something more...dynamic—like the wallpaper could be a looped video or something. It's a little less dynamic than that, unfortunately, but still a cool feature.

So what is it? Well, the wallpaper on your desktop will change, but it's a little slower. Basically, the wallpaper changes appearance depending on what time of day it is. So in Apple's example, there's an image of the Mojave desert; in the morning it's bright and throughout the day it gets darker.

To use it, make sure you have Location Series on—the OS has to know what time it is in your time zone.

THIS OS IS STACKED

Mac excels in many ways; one of the biggest ways is in how it keeps you organized. Apple is always working hard thinking about how to help you stay organized and keep all your content structured in a way that makes it easy to find.

Apple is a bit like a library; other OSes are a bit like used bookstores. Both places have the same thing: books. But one is organized in a way to help you find what you need quickly; the other is organized in a way where you really need to browse for things.

If your desktop looks a little like the below image, then Stacks can help.

How does Stacks clean this mess up? When it's enabled, the above screenshot would look a bit like the below one.

Everything is still there, but it's grouped together. All the images, documents, and movies are in one group. If you want to see anything within that group, then just click the thumbnail and it will expand. If you add a new file to your desktop, it's automatically put in the appropriate group.

If you're on your desktop, you can turn it on by clicking and selecting Use Stacks. You can also do this by going into Finder and then choosing Use Stacks. You can also pick how you want things stacked. By default, it's by kind, but you can also stack by date or tag.

If you want to turn it off, repeat the process above but uncheck Use Stacks.

Menu Bar

One of the most noticeable differences between Windows and Mac on the desktop is the top menu bar. I'll be referring back to this menu bar throughout the book, but right now what you need to know is this bar changes with each program that you open, but some of the features remain the same. The little apple, for instances, never changes—clicking on this will always bring up options to restart, shut down, or log out of your computer. The little magnifying glass at the far right is also always there. Any time you click on that, you can search for files, emails, contacts, etc., that are on your computer.

 Finder File Edit View Go Window Help

Menulets

At the top right, you'll see several "menulets," which include Bluetooth, wireless connectivity, volume, battery, time and date, the name of the account currently logged in, Spotlight, and Notifications, as well as other assorted third-party icons (if installed).

As this book continues, we'll refer back to this part of the menu.

Dock

Windows has a taskbar on the bottom of the screen, and Mac has a Dock; the Dock is where all your commonly used applications are.

If you see a little dot under the icon, then the program is currently open. If you want to close it, then click the icon with two fingers to bring up the options, and then click Quit.

Removing a program from the Dock is pretty simple—just drag the icon to the Trash and let go. This will not remove the program—it only removes the shortcut. Finder, Trash, and Launchpad are the only programs that you cannot remove.

If you want to add a program to the Dock, then open it; when the icon appears on the Dock, click with two fingers, then go to Options and select Keep in Dock.

TRASH

At the right end of the Dock is the Trash. To delete a folder, file or application, drag the item to the Trash, or right-click (two-finger click) the item and select Move to Trash from the pop-up menu. If you want to eject a disk or drive, such as an iPod or USB flash drive, drag the volume into the Trash. As the volume hovers over the Trash, the icon morphs from a trash can to a large eject button. Release the mouse, and your volume will be safely ejected and can be removed from the computer. To empty the Trash, right-click (click with two fingers) on the Trash icon in the Dock, and select Empty Trash.

You can manage the Trash yourself, but I also highly recommend an app called "Clean My Mac" (https://macpaw.com/cleanmymac); it's a little expensive, but when I use it, it normally helps me free up 1GB of storage just by deleting installation files and extensions that I don't need.

APP BUTTONS

The little lights in the image above have no name. Some people call them traffic lights. You'll start seeing a lot of them because nearly all Mac programs use them. On a Windows, you've seen them as an X and a minus in the upper right of your screen. On a Mac, they appear in the upper left of the running program. The red light means close, the yellow light means minimize, and the green makes the app full screen.

Full screen means the program takes up the entire screen and even the Dock disappears. You can see the Dock and other programs quickly by swiping the Trackpad to the right with four fingers. To get back to the app, swipe with four fingers to your left.

LAUNCHPAD

Launchpad is essentially the Start menu on a Windows computer. It shows your programs.

When you click it, you'll see rows of programs; you can immediately start typing to search for an app, or you can just look for it. If you have a lot of apps, then you probably have more than one screen. Swipe with two fingers to the left to see the next screen.

Launchpad takes a lot of cues from iPhone and iPad. If you want to remove a program, for example, you do it the same way you remove an iPhone or iPad app. Just click and hold until an X appears above it, then click the X to remove it. Similarly, to rearrange icons, use the same method for rearranging iPhone / iPad apps—click and hold over the icon until it begins to shake, and then move it wherever you want it to go. You can even put programs into groups the same way as an iPhone / iPad—click and hold over the icon, then drag it on top of the app you want to group it with; finally, when the folder appears, you can let go.

After you delete a program, you can re-download it anytime, by going into the App Store (as long as you downloaded it from the App Store and not from a website).

NOTIFICATIONS

For the past few updates, Apple has attempted to replicate iOS (iPad / iPhone) features; the move is meant to make using a Mac much like using a mobile device. This attempt at replicating features is especially true with Catalina OS.

Notification was a new feature to OS X Yosemite. You can find it on the top menu button at all times; it's to the far right-hand corner and looks like this:

Click it any time you want to see alerts. You can also access it by swiping with two fingers to the left from the edge of your Trackpad.

When you swipe down from the top of an iPad or iPhone you will get a similar screen. There are two parts of the Notifications menu: Today and Notifications.

The Today tab is where you'll see things happening more in the moment—what's the weather, what's in your calendar, what's going on with your stocks, etc. The Notifications tab is where you'll see things like Facebook messages or emails. Later in this book, I'll show you how to customize it.

Split View

Split view is perhaps the biggest added feature to OS X. It lets you run two apps side-by-side—but there's a catch: not all apps are compatible. So if you're scratching your head because this feature won't work for you, then chances are it's not that you are doing it wrong—it's that the app doesn't support the feature.

There are two ways to get the split view to work. Let's look at both of them. First, make sure the two apps that you want to run side-by-side are not running in full screen mode.

Method 1

Click and hold the green button in the upper left corner of your app.

A transparent blue box will appear; drag and drop the app into it (by default, the blue is on the left side, but if you drag to the right side, it will also turn blue and you can drop it in).

Next, click the program you want to use side-by-side.

A side-by-side window now appears; you can use the middle black line to make one bigger or smaller, by dragging left or right.

To return to the normal view, click the green button in the upper left corner of the app once more (you can also hit the ESC key on your keyboard).

Method 2

As you are probably noticing, most things in OS X can happen by several different methods; side-by-side view has two. The second way to get apps is to open your Mission Control, and drag the app to the top menu.

You'll notice, a grey box appears and the box appears to split.

Once you drop the app into that box, you'll see a side-by-side pre-view. Once you click the preview, it will maximize.

Returning to the non-split screen is done the same way as Method 1 (click the green box in the upper left corner or hit the ESC key on the keyboard).

TABBED SOFTWARE

If you've ever used Tabs on Internet Explorer or Chrome, then this next feature might interest you. It allows you to open documents (such as Maps and Pages) with tab viewing. Note: not all Mac apps support this feature.

To use it, open two windows of the same app. I'll use Maps in the example below.

Next, go to Window and Merge All Windows.

Your windows should now be merged.

PICTURE-IN-PICTURE VIDEO

If you'd like to watch a video while you work, then you're in luck! If you already own the video (a video you purchased on iTunes, for example), then just start playing the video and go to View and Float on Top.

But what about Web videos? Such as Vimeo and YouTube? That's easy too. Just double-click the video you are watching, and select Enter Picture-In-Picture.

Your video will immediately begin playing above other windows.

USING NOTES

If you are new to Apple, then the obvious question on your mind might be: why Notes? What is it good for and when should you use it?

Notes is probably *not* what you want to use to write this year's Christmas Newsletter or create a flier for your lost puppy; Notes really excels when you want to create a shared list, jot down school notes, or do something that doesn't need a lot of formatting.

Notes really shines when you sync it with your iPhone; with your iPhone sync'd, you can write your notes, then use your phone to insert a sketch or image.

Once you have created your Note, you can add it to a folder and everything is searchable, which makes it a very organized way of tracking things.

THE NOTES CRASH COURSE

To open it, go to the Launchpad icon on your Dock and click the Notes icon.

Notes, like most of the apps in Catalina, syncs to your iPhone and iPad as long as you are logged into the same iCloud account.

Unlike word processing editors that you may be used to, there is no fancy ribbon or menu bar with lots of features. There's a side bar with a list of all your notes (across devices if you use an iPhone / iPad sync'd to your Mac).

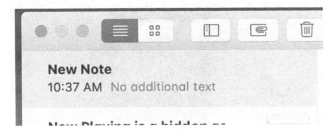

On the top is a very basic menu bar.

VIEWS

The first option next to the app resize options (the red / yellow / green dots) is the view toggle.

This toggle switches between a list view of your notes and a thumbnail view (see below).

If you are in list view, then you only need to click the Note one time to open it; if you are in thumbnail view, then you will need to double click it.

FOLDERS

The next button is for creating folders.

This brings up a list of all your folders (if any).

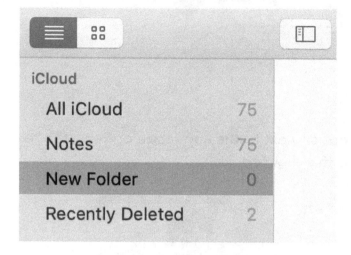

If you don't have one yet, then click New Folder at the bottom of the window.

To rename, delete, or add people to the folder, click the three dots with the circle around them.

Finally, to add a note to a folder, click it from the side, and then drag it into the desired folder.

Once you are done, click the view button again to hide the folders panel.

VIEWING ATTACHMENTS

The next option looks like the button to attach things; that's not correct. It's the option to view all the attachments you have added into notes. When you click on it, you can sort by all the different attachment types (Photos & Videos, Scans, Maps, Websites, Audio, and Documents)

When you double click an attachment, it opens a preview of it (it does *not* open the note which it's found in). If you would like to see the Note that it is in, then right click to bring up the option menu and click "Show in Note."

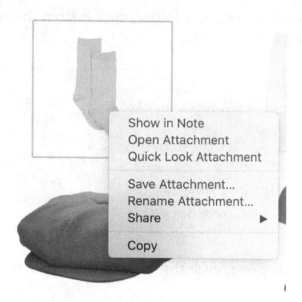

DELETE NOTE

The next option is pretty straightforward. It deletes the note that you have currently selected.

CREATING A NOTE

Next to the delete button is the "Create a Note" button, which, as you can expect, creates a note. When you open your note, the left panel will have the name of the note with a time stamp, and the right will have an empty text area to write in. The title of the note will change once you start typing text; the first line of text is the title of your note. You cannot rename the title; if you change the first line of text in the note, then the title is changed automatically.

LOCK NOTE

The security on Notes may not seem quite as robust as other word processors, but there is a very resourceful Lock feature that helps keep private notes secure and for your eyes only. To use it, click the Lock icon.

This will bring up a dialog box that asks you to add a password. Now anytime you want to open the Note, you'll need a password. If you forget your password then you will not be able to access your Note, so be careful!

Create a password for all your locked notes.

Password:	required
Verify:	required
Password Hint:	recommended

IMPORTANT: If you forget this password, you won't be able to view your locked notes. Learn more...

Cancel   Set Password

CREATE A TABLE

You can also add Tables to your Note. Personally, I would stick to adding tables into other word processing suites, because this is one feature a bit more cumbersome than other tools out there. But if you want to try it out, click the Tables icon.

This adds a very small table to your note—just two rows and two columns.

To add a row or column, click the three little dots on top of the column or to the left of the row, then click what you want to add. You can also delete it using this method.

CREATE A CHECKLIST

If you are using Notes to create a shared list between people (or just a list for yourself), click the Check icon.

This turns each line of text into a list. Hitting return on your keyboard will create a new list item; hitting return twice will take it out of list mode and return it to normal typing.

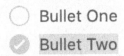

You can click inside any of the circles and check an item off. If you made a mistake, then just uncheck it again.

You can also move a list item up or down by right clicking it, then going to "Move List Item."

By right clicking, you can also go to More and check off all items (or uncheck all items).

ADD A STYLE

While you can't do as much to the format as you could in other word processors, Notes does have basic styles. To access them, click the Aa icon.

This gives you a drop-down of all the possible styles available.

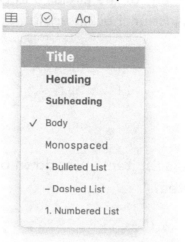

ADDING SKETCHES AND IMAGES

One of the many areas Apple has always really shined is with syncing between devices. Using Notes for Mac with your iPhone, you can add in sketches or take photos.

To get started, go to the photos icon. This brings down a drop down of all your options. You can, of course, add any photo on your Mac with the Photos option.

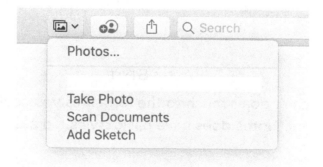

Using the next three options (Take Photo, Scan Documents, Add Sketch) will bring up an image that asks you to connect to your phone to complete the tasks (make sure you are on the same network).

When you add a sketch, you draw it on your phone.

Once you hit done on your phone, it will automatically appear in Notes for Mac.

ADDING COLLABORATORS

If you want to add others to your note, click the icon with the person and +.

Next click "Note 'New Note'".

It will ask how you want to add them. Through messages, a link, AirDrop, etc.

When you're ready, click share, but before you do, click the Permissions drop-down and make sure it's set up the way you want. You can either let the note be view-only for others or you can let them make changes.

SHARING NOTES

If you want to share the note without adding the person to the note, click the share icon.

Next, pick how you would like to share the note.

Searching Notes

The last option on the toolbar is the search box. This lets you search all of your notes for different keywords. For example, whenever I go somewhere with a public Wi-Fi, I add the network key to a Wi-Fi password note (I don't recommend this for sensitive passwords); whenever I need to quickly find it, I search for "WiFi" and it comes up immediately.

Exporting Notes

Now that we've seen all the features on the toolbar, let's go up one level to the top menu bar. Everything you did in the toolbar, you can also do there; there are also, however, a few extra features.

The first is exporting a Note as a PDF. That's found under File > Export as PDF.

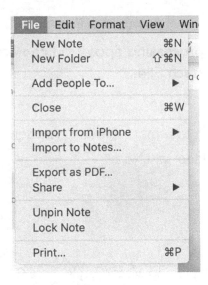

Above Export is the Import option; personally, I find it easier just to share a note from another device, but if you have a copy somewhere and have a reason to import it, then you would go here.

PINNING NOTES

Pinning notes is a very basic, but useful feature; when you click on a note and then select to Pin it from File > Pin Note, it sticks it at the top of all your notes to make it easier to find.

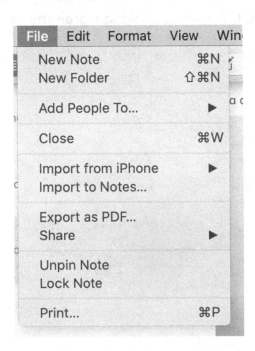

ATTACHING FILES

Unlike many word processing apps, you can actually attach files to Notes. Go to Edit > Attach File.

SPELL CHECK

Like any word processing software, there is a spell checker buried in the top menu. You can start spell check by going to Edit > Spelling and Grammar. By default, it checks spelling / grammar as you type.

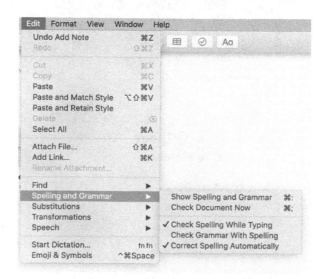

FONT FORMATTER

Finally, while changing the font color / type is not quite as simple as Pages or Word, it is still possible. Go to Format > Font.

[4]

HOW TO FIND THINGS

This chapter will cover:
- Finder
- Gallery view
- Other views in Finder
- Finder tabs
- Tags

One of the greatest things about Mac is how easy it is to find things. Sure, Windows has a search, but it feels clunky and doesn't always work the way you expect. I'll cover how to find things in this chapter.

FINDER

The first icon on your Dock—one of three that cannot be deleted or moved—is the Finder icon.

Finder is the Mac equivalent of Explorer on a Windows computer; as the name implies, it finds things. Finder is pretty resourceful and powerful so this section will be a little longer than others because there's a lot you can do with it.

Let's get started by clicking on the Finder icon.

FINDER REIMAGINED

Finder is how you find things on a Mac—clever name, right? Like a lot of things in MacOS, there are similarities between how it works on Mac and iPhone. Mojave added a few new features still present in Catalina you should know about, however.

Gallery View

There are several different types of views in Finder (where you find things—like File Explorer in Windows). Examples of views are: list, columns, and icons. Gallery view was a new view in Mojave that you still see in Catalina.

Gallery view displays a large preview of the file with thumbnails of everything else in the directory below it. And by "preview" this isn't just for images where you can see what the image looks like—this works across all kinds of docs. If it's a PDF, for example, you can see a preview of the PDF.

To the right of the file, there's a side panel that will tell you the more detailed metadata for the file.

Quick Actions

Apple is all about efficiency; to be more efficient, it helps to be able to do things a little quicker. That's where Quick Actions help. With Quick Actions, you can, for example, change the orientation of a file or add password protection. The actions available depend on the type of file.

OTHER VIEWS

There are four other ways to view folders on your Mac—icons, lists, columns, and Cover Flow. Different views make sense for different file types, and you can change the view using the View Options icons (pictured below).

Cover Flow View

Cover Flow lets you quickly go through thumbnails / previews of photos (it's a little like Film Strip in Windows); you can also sort any of the columns by clicking on the header—so if you are looking for a larger file, then click the Size column, or if you are looking for a recent file, then pick the Date Modified column.

Icon View

Icon View can help if you need to sort through several image files or applications. It gives you either a thumbnail of each picture or an icon for each file or app.

List View

List View, on the other hand, gives you more information about the file, including the date it was last modified. This is the perfect view for sorting.

Column View

Finally, Column View which is kind of a hybrid of List View and Cover Flow View. It shows the folder hierarchy a file is located in. Notice that Finder doesn't include the Windows "go up one level" button—Column View is a good way to get the same results and navigate easily through your file structure.

SORTING IN FINDER

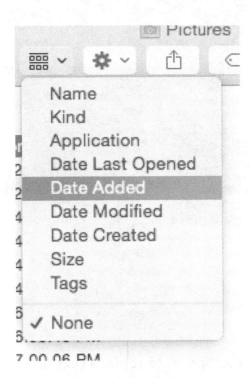

Finder gives you a number of ways to sort your files and folders. You can sort by name, type, the application required for opening the file (like Microsoft Word, for example), the date the file was created, modified, or opened, the file size, and any tags you may have applied.

FILE MANAGEMENT

Most file management tasks in OS X are similar to Windows. Files can be dragged and dropped, copied, cut and pasted. If you need to create a new folder, use the Gear icon in Finder, which will give you the option you need.

Catalina also allows you to batch rename files (i.e. rename several files at once instead of one at a time), potentially saving you hours of time, depending on your file system. To take advantage of this, select the files you'd like to rename (hint: use Command-click to select multiple files, or use Command-A to select everything). Then right-click (two-finger click) the selected files and choose "Rename X Items."

You'll then have the option to replace text or to add text to the file names.

FAVORITES

If you look on the left side of the Finder Window, you'll see a Favorites sidebar. This section includes high-frequency folders, like Documents, Pictures, Downloads, and more.

To add an application or file to your Favorites menu, just drag it over to the Favorites area and drop it. To remove an item from Favorites, right-click it (click with two fingers) and select Remove From Sidebar.

TABBED BROWSING

Apple took a page from Internet browsers by adding something called "Tabbed Browsing" to Finder. Basically, instead of having several Finder boxes open (which is how you had to do it in older OSes) you open tabs. To open an additional Finder tab, press Command-T or click File and New Tab.

If you want to merge all of your tabbed windows, just click Windows in the file menu on the top of your screen, and then Merge All Windows.

Tags

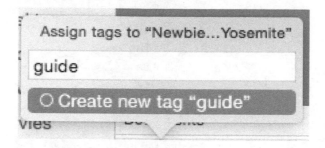

If you use photo apps like Flickr, then you probably know all about tagging; it's essentially adding subjects to your file to make it easier to find. Let's say the file is regarding the 2015 tax year—you can add a tag to the file called "2015 Taxes" or whatever you want it to be. You can also color code it.

To assign a tag to a file (you can also assign it to a folder), click the file / folder with two fingers, and then click tags; if this is your first tag just type it in and hit Enter; if you've already tagged a file and want to use the same name, then click the name of the tag as it appears.

[5]

SURFING THE INTERNET ON MAC

This chapter will cover:
- Setting up Internet
- Browsing with Safari
- Setting up and sending email

The Mac is a beautiful machine, but you can only admire that desktop for so long; eventually, you'll want to get on the Internet—how else will you get your daily dose of cat memes or keep in touch with the Nigerian prince trying to give you money? I'll show you how in this chapter.

There are two methods: Ethernet (i.e. plugging in a LAN cable to your computer) and Wireless.

SETTING UP WITH ETHERNET

All new Mac computers are set up with Wi-Fi; iMacs also have Ethernet ports to plug in a network cable. This option isn't available on any of the Mac laptops—though you can buy an adapter if you absolutely must have it.

If you have a basic Internet modem, then set up is pretty easy. Just plug a network cable into your Internet hub, and plug the other end into your Mac. Once it's plugged in, the Internet should work.

Newer Macs come with top of the line wireless radios for Wi-Fi, so you should be perfectly fine without using the Ethernet port.

SETTING UP WIRELESS NETWORKS

Setting up a wireless connection is also pretty simple. Just click the Wi-Fi menu on the menu bar. It looks like the image below and is near the upper right corner:

As long as there's a wireless network in range, it will show up when you click it (sometimes it does take a few seconds to appear).

If there's a lock next to the Wi-Fi name, then you'll need to know the passcode (if it's a home Internet connection, then it's usually on the bottom of your Internet modem; if it's at a business, then you'll have to ask for the code. If there's no lock, then it's an open network. You usually see this kind of network at places like Starbucks.

If it's a locked network, then as soon as you click on it, it will ask for the code; once it's entered and you click Connect, then you're connected (assuming you added it right); if it's not locked then once you click on it, it will attempt to connect.

Airport Express / Airport Extreme

If you need more range in your wireless connection or want to set up a private network, Apple sells two Mac accessories. One is the Airport Express ($99) and the other is the Airport Extreme ($199, or $299 to $399 if you'd like the one with a hard drive).

The Express is a good option for people wanting to add a private network (so, for instance, you can have a network just for guest and guest printing); the Airport Extreme gives excellent range; I use one in my home because the modem supplied with my phone company could barely reach the next room over and the signal strength was weak; the Extreme not only got to the next room, but it got several more rooms—I can now get a signal more than 100 feet from where the Extreme is located. It's a pretty easy installation, and Apple has videos for those who need extra help.

The more expensive models are also a good option for backing up computers. The $299 and $399 models offer up to 3TB of storage; the way it works is your computer connects to it, and will back up your computer in the background, so your computer is always being backed up. These models also let you share files. So, for instance, if you want a private storage locker for anyone who connects to your network, then you could do so here.

Safari

Just as a Windows computer has Internet Explorer as the default web browser, Mac has Safari as the default web browser; if you've used Safari on your iPhone or iPad then you should already be accustomed to it.

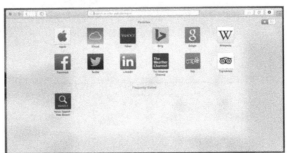

Noticeably absent from Safari is something called "Flash". Flash is what you might have used to watch some videos and other web apps; you can always download it, but this will affect the battery life of your laptop, as Flash tends to drain the battery quickly—which is one of the reasons Apple does not include it. You can download it from Adobe if it's essential to your searching; just Google "Flash for safari browser" to get the free download.

One of the biggest advantages of using Safari over another web browser is a feature called Handoff. Let's say you're reading an article on your phone on the subway coming into work, and when you get to work and want to pick up where you left off on a larger Mac screen. Just open up Safari, then click the two square boxes in the upper right corner.

If your iPhone or iPad is synced with the computer, then you'll see its name and the pages that it's currently browsing. It's not the most obvious feature—you might miss it the first time you try it, but it's there. It's at the bottom; it will have a cloud with your device's name and then the webpage under it. Click the webpage name and it will launch the page.

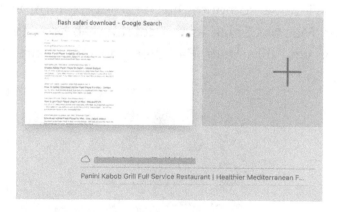

You can also handoff a Mac page to your iPhone or iPad in the same way.

In addition to websites, Handoff also lets you seamlessly sync things like maps, messages, and documents (Pages, Numbers, and Presentation documents).

The Toolbar

So now that you know about Handoff, how do you actually use Safari?

Let's start at the top—literally. Some of these features will probably be more obvious than others, but in the tradition of keeping it simple, I'll cover even the easy stuff.

The first two buttons (the right and left arrows) make the webpage go either forward or back to the previous or next webpage. The button next to this brings up a side panel.

The panel brings up your bookmarks and reading list (we will cover this in a little bit more detail shortly).

Right smack in the middle is the address bar, which doubles as a search bar. What does that mean? It means if you know the webpage you want to go to, you can type it in; but if you want to search for something, just type in the name and it will search for it in whatever search engine you've set up (Google, for example).

Over on the right side, you have your download button (which won't be there if you haven't downloaded any files—or if you've cleared the files that you've downloaded).

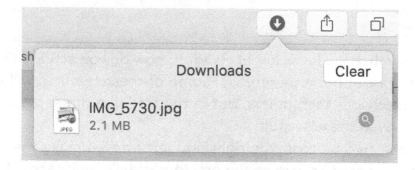

Next to download is the Share button; you can click this button to email the webpage you are currently on. You can also use this button to bookmark a page or add it to your reading list.

The "More..." option under share will bring up a list of possible extensions (I'll cover extensions later in this book).

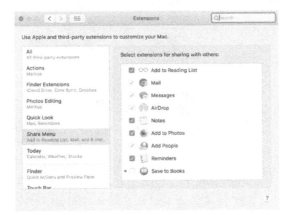

The top toolbar is a bit…bare; there might even be options on there that you don't want. If you right click (or click with two fingers) on your trackpad, you'll see an option that says Customize.

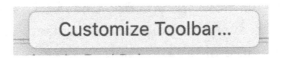

This brings up all kinds of things you can put in your toolbar. It also puts the toolbar into edit mode so you can drag stuff (or move stuff) off your toolbar that you don't want.

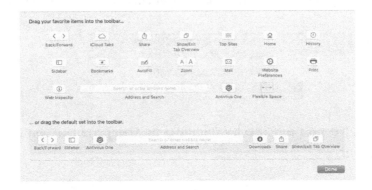

Once you click what you want on your toolbar, you can drag it to where you want it to go. If there's something on the toolbar that you don't want, just drag it down and let go.

ALL ABOUT TABS

Tabs probably are nothing new to you. They are a standard feature on every popular Internet browser. Tabs let you have multiple webpages open in the same window—so you don't have to have several windows open. It helps keep everything nice and organized.

Below is an example of tab browsing.

Alternatively, below is an example of having them in windows instead.

You can open a new tab by clicking on the plus button (+) to the right of the tab bar.

If you click and hold that button, you can also bring up a list of all your recently visited webpages.

Just like you could right click on the toolbar to see more options, you can also right click on the tab bar. The option I find most helpful is Close Other Tabs—this quickly closes all your opened tabs.

PRIVATE WINDOW

If you go up to the top menu, and click file, you'll see a little option called "New Private Window." It's a very useful (and misunderstood) feature, so let's talk about it.

At its core, New Private Window is like an isolated Internet session where nothing is remembered. So if you type in "I love Smurfs" there's no record of it! It looks just like a normal browser window but it's a different shade and has a message about it being in private mode.

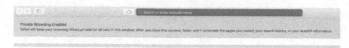

Easy enough, right? Well this is where it gets tricky. Because just because it says "private" that doesn't mean it is "private." If someone had installed a keystroke tracker on your computer, for example, then it would still be able to track what you are doing. Hopefully no one has installed a keystroke tracker on your computer though!

More importantly, however, is that just because the browser isn't keeping track of what you are doing doesn't mean your computer or server is also ignoring everything—those things are quite nosy! If you are on a work computer using private mode, for example, your employer could still monitor you. If you are on a home computer and you are downloading a file that is illegal, your IP will know what you are doing.

What's the lesson here? Don't do anything stupid (or illegal) because you think your session is private.

So why use private mode at all? Personally, I use it for things that I don't want cookies to track—for example, I want to shop on some website for my wife's birthday; I don't want my wife to sit at the computer and see that I was shopping on some site for her birthday! If I had to do banking on a public computer, then I'd also use this mode because it's safer than the other.

A History of You

Your browser keeps a pretty long record of what you are doing—unless you are in Private Mode. That can be both a blessing and a curse.

If you are ever on a public computer or just want to erase your history for whatever reason, then click Safari > Clear History.

If you'd like to see what's actually in your History, then just click on History in your top menu.

From History you'll see your recent history, but can also click Show All History. This is helpful for two reasons. One, you can see your history by date. So let's say you can't remember some article you read, but you know what date you read it on. You can drill down to that date and see everything you looked at.

History

Website	Address
▶ 🕘 Last Visited Today	171 items
▶ 🕘 Tuesday, February 4, 2020	328 items
▶ 🕘 Monday, February 3, 2020	228 items
▶ 🕘 Sunday, February 2, 2020	76 items
▶ 🕘 Saturday, February 1, 2020	240 items
▶ 🕘 Friday, January 31, 2020	343 items
▶ 🕘 Thursday, January 30, 2020	295 items
▶ 🕘 Wednesday, January 29, 2020	487 items
▶ 🕘 Tuesday, January 28, 2020	67 items
▶ 🕘 Monday, January 27, 2020	178 items
▶ 🕘 Sunday, January 26, 2020	117 items

Over on the right side, you can also search your history. So, for example, you want to see everything you read from NYTimes.com, then you can search for that term and see everything.

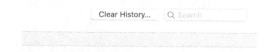

Bookmarks / Reading List

I've quickly covered how to add webpages to your bookmarks and reading list. Let's look at it in more detail.

Reading List is the easiest, so let's start there. When you add something to your reading list, you are telling Safari you want to read it later. You can put anything here, but ideally, it's best suited for articles.

Once they're in your reading list, you can right click on any name to see a list of options; if you happen to be syncing with your phone, you can Save Offline to read it when you don't have data. You can also go here to remove an article.

When you bookmark something, there are a few more options. You'll get a dialog box and the first option is favorites.

When you open a new tab, you'll see the favorites right up on top. These are basically your go-to websites that you are always going to, so it's best to keep the list somewhat short; you can click any of those icons to move them around.

If you click the drop down in the previously shown dialog box, then you'll see all the possible folders for your bookmarks (if you have any), or you can just stick it in the general bookmarks folder.

Once you open the bookmarks sidebar, you can right click on any entry to bring up options—including deleting or renaming the bookmark.

You can also create a bookmark folder here. Once you create a folder, you can immediately name it (or you can name it later by right clicking and bringing up the options menu).

Once you have a bookmark folder, you can drag any of your bookmarks into it to stay organized.

EXPORTING

The bad thing about the Internet is it's always changing; the article you read yesterday may not be there tomorrow. Printing is nice to have a record of something...if you like to waste paper and ink.

The better option is to export it as a PDF and then store it on your computer; this will work great for articles and standard web entries. If you try and do this with something with some sort of JavaScript (a report, for example), then you probably won't like the results.

To try it, go to File > Export as PDF.

READER MODE

A few years back, Safari released a nice feature called Reader Mode. As the name suggest, this gives you a more reader-friendly version of what you are reading online.

Here's an example of a normal article:

And here's that same article in Reader Mode:

The mode helps eliminate some of the common flashy ad distractions you can see on websites. It works great for blogs and other online publications, but it's not for everything—you won't see this mode, for example, while you are shopping online.

If the mode is available, then you will see a little paragraph button in your top toolbar. Click it to enable this mode.

You can also access this view (when available) under View > Show Reader.

EMOJI THAT

Chances are at some point you will want to send an email with an Emoji. Just whip on out the Emoji keyboard, right? Not exactly. This is possible on your mobile device, but it's a bit different on a desktop or laptop. It's still pretty easy, however.

When you are ready to add an Emoji, just go to Edit > Emoji & Symbols from your top menu.

This will bring up a dialog box with all the possible Emoji's. Once you see the one you want, just click it.

FIND IT

Have you ever searched for something on Google, then gone to the page and wondered where on earth it is in the result for that term? You can go to Edit > Find and search for the term to see where exactly the term comes up on the page; you can also hit Command F on your keyboard to do this.

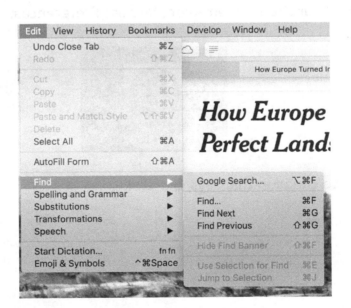

WHAT'S UP DOCK?

Down in your dock bar, there's a final list of options. Just click with two fingers on your trackpad while your finger is over the Safari icon.

DEFAULT BROWSER

What if you want to use Safari, but you don't want it to be your default browser? That's an easy fix.

Go to the Launchpad, then select System Preferences.

Next, go to the icon that says General.

This will bring up a box with a few options; one of them says "Default web browser." Click that and select what browser you want. If you want Firefox or Chrome, but don't see it, then you need to download it first. It will only show the browsers that you have installed.

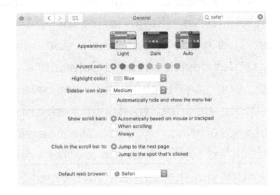

IMPORTING BOOKMARKS

Starting something new is never fun; if you've been a Chrome or Firefox user, then all those bookmarks you've been collecting for years will not be there.

You can easily move them over, however. Click File > Import From, and select where you want to grab the bookmarks from.

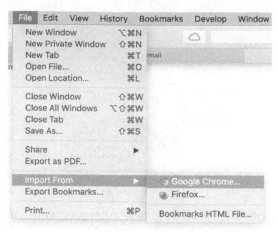

SAFARI FOR WINDOWS

If you are an iPhone / iPad user trapped in a Windows world, then I have unfortunate news for you: Safari is not for you—at least not on your desktop computer. This guide will still help you with using the browser on your mobile or tablet device running Safari.

Having said that, you can "technically" get Safari for Windows. Several years back, Apple decided to make a stronger push to get the browser in front of more users; they released several versions of Safari for Windows but decided to discontinue it after version 5.

So, while you *cannot* get the current version of Safari on Windows, if you do a Google search for Safari, you will be able to find older version. My recommendation is not to put Safari on your Windows computer for two reasons: one, it's not supported and what you are downloading is a very old and unstable version; and two, you are downloading it unofficially from other websites so you are opening your computer up to vulnerabilities.

The same is also true if you have an Android phone or Chromebook; there has never been a version of Safari for Chrome OS, but there are plenty of browsers that try and clone the experience. Again, however, my recommendation is to stay away from these; they are from lesser-known companies.

SAFARI EXTENSIONS

Extensions extend the capabilities of your browser; think of them like apps for your browser.

FIND EXTENSIONS

The one unfortunate thing about Safari is that other browsers have a lot more extensions to pick from; the good thing about it, however, is that the ones you find have been vetted and are much better quality.

You can find Extensions by clicking on Safari > Safari Extensions.

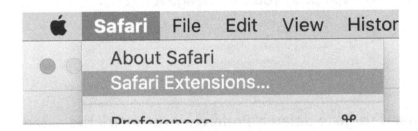

This opens up the App Store and immediately shows you extensions. You can also search the App Store if you know the extension's name.

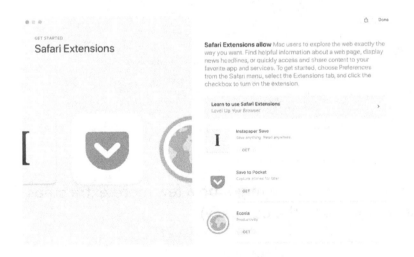

ADD AN EXTENSION

To add an extension, find the one you want, and then click the blue Get button

Once it's installed, it will probably give you a popup about allowing notifications. Whatever you pick, you can change it later.

Next, you'll need to go to Safari > Preferences and click the extensions tab. Find the extension you want to use, and check it off.

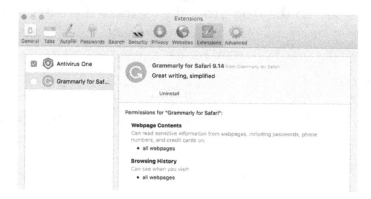

Depending on the extension, there might be a few more extra steps (such as creating an account with the company).

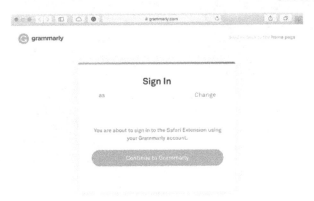

USING EXTENSIONS

Some extensions will work behind the scenes and you will rarely notice them; others are more in the foreground.

Earlier in the book, I showed you how to customize the top toolbar; you can refer back to this to add your extension onto the toolbar.

UNINSTALLING EXTENSIONS

To uninstall an extension, go to Safari > Extensions, then click the Extensions tab. From here, click the uninstall button.

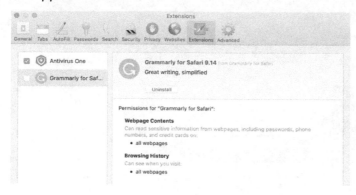

PRIVACY AND SECURITY

The Preference Menu (found by going to Safari > Preferences) contains all the adjustments that you can make within Safari. This section will walk you through what's found in each.

GENERAL

General is where you can tell Safari what you want to show when you open the app. When you open a new tab, for example, do you want it to show your favorite websites (the default setting) or something else? You can also tell it where you want downloads to go and when to delete your history.

TABS

There aren't a lot of settings here—just toggles to turn on and off shortcut commands.

AUTOFILL

AutoFill is letting Safari remember certain things you type in forms. The setting here you may want to use is "Other Forms." If you click the edit button, you can remove websites that have your autofill info stored. For example, if you no longer want Safari to remember your username for a particular website, then you can go in here and delete it.

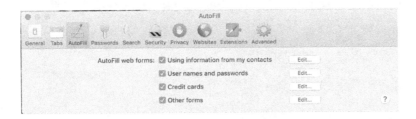

Passwords

Similar to autofill, Passwords remembers your passwords for certain websites. So if you decide that you no longer want your password remembered for a shopping website, then you can go in here and delete just that one particular store.

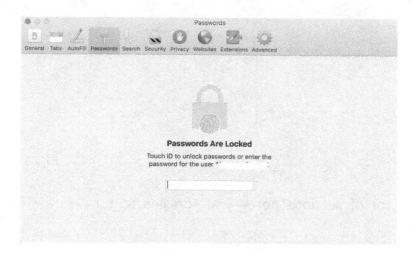

Search

Search lets you change the browser's default search engine (Google) to another search engine—such as Bing, Yahoo, or DuckDuckGo.

Security

Security is just a very simple toggle menu. By default, both are checked off.

PRIVACY

Privacy is where you go to turn on and off cookies.

WEBSITES

Websites lets you pick what websites can access certain things on your website. For example, can Facebook access your Webcam or can Google maps access your location?

If you ever see those popups that say "Allow or Deny" on your Mac, this is where you can change whatever you picked.

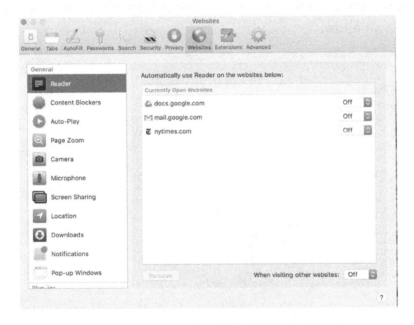

EXTENSIONS

I've walked through what's found in Extensions earlier in this book.

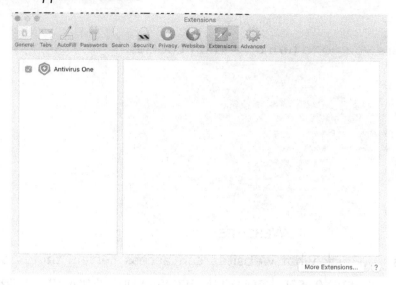

ADVANCED

Finally, advanced contains features that you probably will never use (such as encoding).

There is a helpful accessibility section that lets you pick the smallest font size that you will allow.

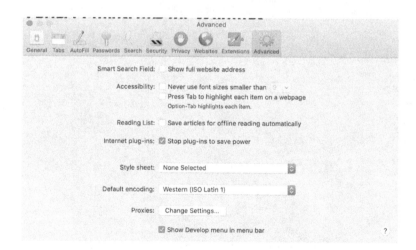

SAFARI PREFERENCES

If your computer is in a place where other people can get to it, or if you are just generally concerned about your privacy being violated, then head on over to Privacy and Security in the System Preferences.

CREATING STRONG PASSWORDS

Strong passwords are the first line of defense against potential hackers (or smart children!); a strong password is not something like "password"; a strong password has letters, numbers and even symbols in it. It could be something like this: "@mY_MACb00k."

You can use the Password Assistant to test how strong your password is.

When Keychain loads, you will be able to view the entire list of accounts that are already synced to your Keychain. If you would like to change the password for an account that already exists, find the account and double-click on it. If not, click on the '+' button at the bottom to add a new account.

When the new window comes up, take a look at the bottom. There will be a field for password, and at the right of it will be a small key icon. Click the key icon to open up Password Assistant.

From Type you can select Manual (create your own), Memorable, Letters & Numbers, Numbers Only, Random, and FIPS-181 compliant.

Suggestions will automatically populate, and you can scroll through several different suggestions by using the dropdown menu.

Adjust the length slider to make the password longer or shorter. Any password you create will meet at least these requirements to be considered fair.

As you generate a password, the quality indicator will change to show you how safe and complex a given password is.

FIREWALL

Another line of defense you can add is a firewall, which protects you from unwanted connections to potentially malicious software applications, websites, or files.

To enable the firewall that comes with your Mac, go to System Preferences > Security & Privacy and select the Firewall tab. Before you can make any changes, click on the lock icon in the bottom left corner and enter your administrator password to continue.

FIND MY MAC

Just like your iPhone or iPad, Mac comes with a handy feature called "Find My Mac" which lets you find your computer if someone steals it or you misplace it; you can also wipe its hard drive clean remotely.

To enable Find My Mac, go to System Preferences > iCloud and check the box next to Find My Mac. Your location services must also be turned on, so go to System Preferences > Security & Privacy > Privacy > Location Services and make sure Enable Location Services is checked on.

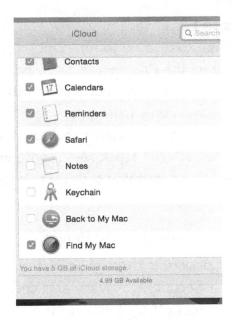

To track your computer, you can log into any computer and visit iCloud.com, enter your iCloud login information, and click on Find My Mac. As long as the Mac is awake and connected to the Internet through Wi-Fi or Ethernet, you will be able to play a loud sound, lock it, or completely erase it so your private information is removed.

PRIVACY

Apple knows people worry about privacy; they have lots built in to help you control what can (and can't) be seen.

INTERNET PRIVACY

If you'd like to clear your search and browsing history, there are two ways to do it: either by clicking on Safari > Clear History and Website Data or History > Clear History and Website Data. Both can be found on the top menu bar. When the window comes up, you will be able to choose how far back you want the clearing to reach. Once you make a selection, just press the Clear History button to make the changes final.

Cookies allow websites to store data and track certain things, like what other websites you visit during your Internet session, or what kind of products you tend to look at the most. This information is mostly used by advertisers to better target ads for you, but the option is always there if you'd like to disable them. Open up Safari, go to Safari > Preferences, then select the Privacy tab. The cookie options range from allowing all websites to store cookies to blocking all websites. You can also allow cookies only from your most frequently visited websites. If you prefer not to be tracked, check off the box at the bottom that says Ask Websites To Not Track Me. Some websites will not function as you may want them to if you disable this feature.

APPLICATION PRIVACY

The other part of privacy is through installed applications. Go to System Preferences > Security & Privacy and click the Privacy tab. You can shut Location Services off by checking the box next to Enable Location Services. Browse through the left sidebar and you'll be able to customize permissions. If you don't want any apps to access your contacts or calendars, here is where you can block some or all programs from that information.

SCREEN TIME

Screen Time might be something you are familiar with. It's been on iPads and iPhones for a while. It comes to MacOS with the Catalina update. What is it? It's a productivity setting that lets you restrict how long you can use certain apps (games for instance). It's highly customizable, so you can set one app like Word to have zero restrictions, but another one like Internet to have limits.

Screen Time isn't an app in the traditional sense; it's an app within your system settings. To use it, go to System Preferences, then click Screen Time.

This launches a new window that tells you how much time you've been on your computer.

You can set up a passcode by clicking on options at the bottom of the window.

App Limits is where you can start restricting certain apps. Click the '+' in this section.

From here select the app (or kinds of apps) that you want to limit.

At the bottom, you can say how much time you want to set the limit to.

Under Always Allow, you can select apps that have no restrictions.

MAIL

Mail is the Mac equivalent of Outlook; like Safari, it works in a very similar way to iPad and iPhone. Apple will provide you with a free email address that ends @icloud.com, but you can also add normal email into the application (like Hotmail, Yahoo, and Gmail).

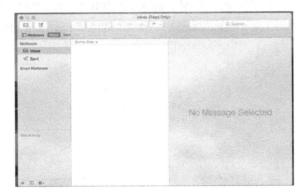

ADDING ACCOUNTS

To get started, you need to add your email account. Locate the Mail app by clicking on Launchpad, and then clicking the Mail app icon.

Once the app opens, go to the top menu bar and click Mail > Add Account. This will load the Add Account dialogue box.

Select the provider that you will be adding in (Note: you can go back and add as many accounts as you want) and click Continue. Next, you'll be asked what your Name, Email Address, and Password are.

If you are using a popular email provider, set up is pretty self-explanatory. If you are using a business email, then you will probably need to work with your system administrator to get it added in correctly.

Once it's set up, you should start seeing mail show up on your computer.

SENDING AN EMAIL

Now that you have an account added, you can start sending mail; to send mail you can either press Command-N on your keyboard, go to the top menu and select File and New Message, or click the Compose icon (it looks like a pencil going through a square).

The New Message dialogue box will appear. In the To field, enter the email address or addresses that you'd like to send a message to, add in a subject and message, and then hit the paper airplane in the upper left corner when you are ready to send the message.

You can also add formatting to the message by clicking on the "A" button. Formatting is very basic—you can bold, add italics, underline, and change the coloring.

[6]

THERE'S AN APP FOR THAT

This chapter will cover:
- Phone calls
- Contacts
- iMessage
- FaceTime
- Photo Booth
- Calendar
- Reminders
- Notes
- iTunes
- App Store
- Siri
- Mac meets iOS

Now that you know about how Mac works (and how to find cat memes), I'm going to talk about the pre-installed programs.

PHONE CALLS

Apple products really work best with other Apple products; that's even truer with Catalina, where you can sync your iPhone account to make phone calls (both video and regular) and send messages right from your Mac. Additionally, you can even use your iPhone's data connection to get the Internet on your laptop on the go—this is especially handy while travelling if you don't want to pay for Wi-Fi spots that charge for access (just keep in mind that your data connection does have monthly limits and using a computer can go through those limits very quickly—in other words, this probably isn't something you want to do to stream Netflix movies).

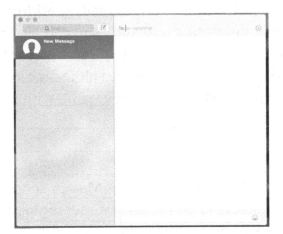

CONTACTS

Unless you are a business person, having contacts on your computer might not seem necessary; here's the advantage of it—it syncs with your phone. So having a contact on your computer will carry over to your other mobile devices. To use it, go to your Launchpad, then click the icon.

Contacts

If you're signed into iCloud, then you should see dozens of contacts already. To create a new contact, click on the (+) button at the bottom of the main window. On the next screen add all the info you want—it can be as much or as little as you desire. Some contacts may only need a website address, others might have mailing address—it's entirely up to you how much information you add. You can also edit a contact by finding their name, then clicking on the Edit button. If you want to delete someone, then find their name and hit Delete on your keyboard (you can also delete by clicking on their name with two fingers).

IMESSAGE

When you use iMessages from your Mac to send messages just keep in mind that it's kind of like instant messaging for Mac users—that means it's designed to work with Mac products...nothing else.

Setting Up iMessage

1. To set up iMessage, click the Messages icon to launch it.
2. If you were already logged into iCloud on the Mac, you will automatically be logged into iMessage.
3. If you'd like to change this account or haven't yet logged in, select Messages > Preferences on the top menu bar.
4. When the Accounts dialogue box comes up, click on the Accounts tab.
5. In the left-hand window, you will see iMessage. Select it.
6. The following screen will prompt you to enter the email address and password associated with iCloud. Do so and click the blue Sign In button to complete the setup process.

Setting Up Other IM Clients

While iMessage is made for Mac products, you can use it for other messaging services like Google, Yahoo, and AOL. To add other instant messaging (IM) clients to Messages:

1. Open up Messages if it isn't already running.
2. On the top menu bar, click Messages > Add Account.

3. Select the type of account that you'd like to add, such as Gmail or Yahoo, and select Continue.
4. You will be prompted to enter the appropriate email address and password, and click the Set Up button to finish.

So now that it's set up, how do you send a message?

Start New Conversation

1. Before we begin, take a look at the entire Messages screen. It should be totally empty with no conversations. On the left sidebar it will say No Conversations. This is where you will be able to change between different conversations with people by clicking on each one. On the right-hand side, you will also see No Conversation Selected. Here is where you will be able to type new messages and read everything in whatever conversation is currently selected. If you have an iPhone (or any phone for that matter), it will be like the screen where you read your text messages.
2. To create a new conversation with someone, click the Compose new message button located at the top of the left sidebar, next to the search bar. It should look a little pencil inside of a square.

When you get a message, if your sound is enabled, you'll get a little chime.

Tapbacks

If you've used Stickers on the iPad and iPhone, you might be disappointed to see that feature has not yet arrived on MacOS. There is one feature from iOS: Tapbacks. Tapbacks let you respond to a message to indicate you like what the message says or that you agree with it. To use it, right-click (two-finger click) on any message and select your response.

FACETIME

FaceTime allows you to connect with friends and family using your computer's built-in camera. I've heard people say they are so worried that someone is watching them through their webcam that they cover it with tape. When FaceTime is in use (i.e. when the camera is on and people can see you) a bright green light comes on—so you don't have to worry about people spying on you...if you don't see the light, then the camera is off.

The app can be launched by clicking on Launchpad > FaceTime.

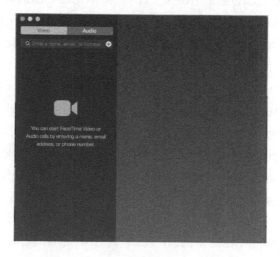

On the left side you can enter a person's name if they are in your Contacts, or a phone number. For FaceTime to work, the other person must also have an Apple device, and accept your call.

You can also use FaceTime audio. This lets you call someone without the camera—it's essentially a Wi-Fi phone call.

PHOTO BOOTH

We're a culture of selfies, so it's appropriate to talk about the app that takes your picture.

To get started, go to Launchpad and click the Photo Booth icon.

Couple of things you should notice once the app loads. First, you! If you look to the top of your screen, there should be a green light. That tells you the camera is on. But now click on a different app in your Dock—see how the green light goes off? And now click on the Photo Booth icon again, and once again the green light is on. What's going on with that light? The light indicates your camera is on—but it only stays on while you are in the Photo Booth app.

Are you ready to take a picture? Put on your silly face and click the camera button.

Like a lot of Apple apps, it's a powerful app with not a lot to it. There are only a handful of options. So let's talk about those options.

First, like a lot of Mac apps, this one can be run in full screen mode; just click the green button in the upper left corner. To exit full screen mode, you can either click the green button again or hit the ESC button on your keyboard. When you are using an app in full screen, you can always get back to your desktop by swiping with three fingers to your right on the Trackpad.

So that first photo was just for fun and now you want to get rid of it. That's really easy; on the bottom of the screen you'll see all of your recent photos. Click the one you want to delete, and hit the X in the corner.

But let's say you really like a photo—so much so that you want to share it with all of your friends. Just click the photo, and then hit the square button with an arrow pointing up, and pick how you want to share it.

There are all sorts of effects for taking photos and videos. Try a few out; just click on the Effects button in the bottom right corner (Note: if you don't see that button then you probably are still viewing your photos, so click the camera button to get back).

Effects

This will bring up 45 different camera effects.

You won't see all 45 at once; you'll see them nine at a time; click the arrows or the circles to see the next nine effects (Note: The last page of effects is for you to add your own backgrounds). When you see the effect you want, just click it.

When you are back to the main screen, there are three options in the lower left corner of the box.

The default box is the middle one. That takes one photo. The first one will take four different photos (one in each box), and the last will take a video of you. When using the video option, the camera will change to a video recorder.

If you want to use some of the fancier effects where it puts you somewhere you aren't (say Yosemite or the beach), then it will ask you to step out of the picture so it can detect the background; then after a few seconds you will step back in. It's best to use a solid background for this effect. If you aren't happy with the way it looks, then you can reset the filter by going to the Menu bar on top, then clicking View and finally clicking Reset Effect.

View	Camera	Window	Help
Show Photo			⌘1
Show Effects			⌘2
Show Last Effect			⌘3
Next Page of Effects			⌘→
Previous Page of Effects			⌘←
Reset Effect			⇧⌘R
Start Slideshow			
Enter Full Screen			^⌘F

If you want to add your own background, then go to the last page of Effects, and drag a photo of your choice into the box. Once you see that photo appear, click on it to activate the effect.

Don't be afraid to play around with the program. There's nothing you can press that will mess anything up!

CALENDAR

Calendar is another feature that can be synced to your iCloud account—so as long as you're using the same account, then everything you put in your calendar from your computer will also show up on your iPhone and iPad. You can also sync the calendar to other ones you may be using online like Google or Yahoo.

To get started with it, go to your Launchpad in the Dock and click on the Calendar icon.

At the top of the application window from left to right you have the standard stoplight buttons, Calendars, New Event (+), several different views including Day and Month, and the Search bar.

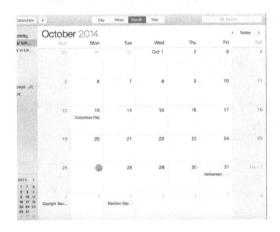

Syncing Calendars

If you already use a calendar with iCloud, Google, Yahoo, or any other provider, you can sync it up with the Mac Calendar application.

1. In the top menu bar click Calendar > Add Account.
2. Like you did with Mail, you'll be prompted to enter your name, email address, and password.

Once you finish the setup process your events from that calendar should automatically populate in the Calendar window. If you have multiple accounts with separate calendars, you can filter through them by clicking on the Calendars button in the toolbar, and checking or unchecking the boxes next to the appropriate calendars.

Changing Views

You can change the calendar view between Day, Week, Month, or Year by clicking on the corresponding button in the toolbar.

Day will display all of that day's events, broken down by hour.

Week will show you the whole week at a glance, and displays blocks for events so you can easily see when you have events, and if you have any upcoming free time.

The Month view will probably be your default view if you just need your calendar to remind you about bill payments and due dates, or don't have too many appointments each month but they are scattered through the month.

REMINDERS

As the name implies, the Reminders application is used to remind you of things—and, as you might have guessed by now, it can be synced using iCloud to the Reminders app on your iPhone or iPad.

The app lets you create lists for things like groceries or anything else on your mind; you can also use the app to schedule when things are due—like paying a bill by the 15th of the month. It can even be set to remind you every time you leave or arrive at your home to turn your home alarm on or off.

You can create shared lists so others in your network can also add things to the list.

To get started, open the app by clicking on the Launchpad icon, then selecting it from the list of apps.

Creating a list is still very simple. Tap Add List from the lower right corner of your screen.

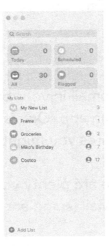

Once you create your first list, you can start adding to it by tapping the '+' button in the upper right corner. This lets you add the item as well as set when it's due and even include images and attachments.

If you tap the ① at any point, you'll be able to add more details (such as a due date or even what location to remind you at—you could, for example, have it remind you when you get to the grocery store).

Tap Return on your keyboard to add another item.

To share a list, right-click (two-finger click) the name and add a person that you want to share it with.

This option also works to remove a list.

MAIL

You may be used to checking your email in your browser. There are a few advantages to emailing through an app. One is instant notifications when mail comes; another is features you might not get in browser-based mail.

If you want to try an app, then there are plenty you can choose from: Airmail, Outlook, Spark, Canary Mail (some are free, some are not).

For this book, I'm going to cover only one app: Apple Mail.

Mail Crash Course

To get started, go to your Launchpad and click the Mail app.

Next, it will ask you to sign into your email provider. The steps vary depending on the services you use, but it will walk you through each step.

Once you have your mail set up, you'll immediately start seeing your inbox fill up with all the messages from that account. Don't see it? Go to "Get New Mail" under Mailbox in the top menu.

The app should look pretty familiar to you because most the features from your browser mail are there.

A few features you should know about:

Block – If there's someone you don't want to hear from, then block them. To do so, open the email from them, click on their name, and select Block Contact from the dropdown. If only blocking people in real-life was that easy!

When you right-click (two-finger click) on a mail message, you also have a few options.

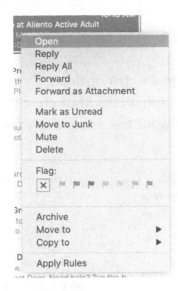

If you have ever used email before, then you will know what Reply, Reply All, etc., do. One that might be new is "Flag." Flag lets you color coordinate different messages to help you find them more easily.

You can also right-click (two-finger click) in the side menu to get more options.

LOCATION BASED REMINDER

If you want to create a reminder that is location-based (i.e. "when I leave work, remind me to call wife") then follow the steps above.

Click the Information icon next to the reminder (the "i" with a circle).

○ Call Wife

This will bring up a few extra options. One says, "remind me" with a checkbox for "At a location"; click that checkbox. Next, enter the address, and select if you want the reminder when you get there or when you're leaving there.

Call Wife

remind me	☐ On a Day
	☑ At a Location
	[_____] ▼
	Enter a contact or an address
	⦿ Leaving ○ Arriving
priority	None
note	None

Done

NOTES

Newer Macs come with Pages preinstalled, so what's the point of Notes? Notes is a more basic program than Pages or Word—you can't do any fancy formatting. The advantage is that it opens and saves quickly. So in short, Notes is for when you just need to jot something down quickly.

To open it, go to the Launchpad icon on your Dock and click the Notes icon.

Notes, like most of the apps in Catalina, syncs to your iPhone and iPad as long as you are logged into the same iCloud account.

CREATING AND EDITING NOTES

1. There are a few different ways to create a brand new note. You can start a new note by clicking on the Compose icon (the square with a pencil going through it), or double-clicking an empty space in the left sidebar. You can also right-click the left sidebar and select New Note.
2. Once the note is created, the line will begin blinking in the right window, indicating that it's time for you to get writing.
3. The notes will automatically save as you type, so exiting Notes won't mean you lose progress.
4. If you need to pick up where you left off on a note, you can use the search bar to find the exact note you are looking for, or scroll through the left sidebar and select the appropriate note. With the note highlighted, click anywhere in the right window to begin editing that note, or double-click to open up a smaller window.
5. To remove notes, find the one you'd like to delete and highlight it. Press the Delete key and confirm it. You can also right-click a note and select Delete.

Notes can be shared through different outlets like LinkedIn, Facebook, Mail, and Messages. If you'd like to share a note, click on the Share button in the top right corner and select how you'd like to send it.

ITUNES IN A NON-ITUNES WORLD

iTunes is a thing on Windows. It's where you buy and manage music, shows and all things content that you bought from Apple. On a Mac? It used to be a thing. In Catalina OS, however, Apple has pulled iTunes apart and made it separate—so if you want to buy music, you now go to Apple Music; if you want to buy videos, you go to Apple TV. The interface is very simple.

I'll cover Apple Music more in the chapter on Apple Services. In this section I'll cover only how to buy music and iTunes Match.

Show the iTunes Store in Apple Music

When you open the Music app, you should see an option in the left menu for the iTunes Store.

When you click on that, it will show you an iTunes Store that looks a lot like the old iTunes app—nearly identical to the one you might be used to if you have an iPad or iPhone.

If you have an Apple Music subscription, then there's a chance that iTunes Store link will be missing—why buy an album if it comes with your subscription, after all? Just because you have a subscription to listen to music for free doesn't mean you won't want to buy anything. If you want to buy an album but don't see the link, then here's what you do:

Go to File > Preferences...

Under the General tab, check off iTunes Store.

After hitting OK, it will show up in your left menu.

How does the store work? Clicking on the Search bar in the top right-hand corner will pull up trending searches in case you are looking for what's hot. If you are looking for a specific song or movie, type it into the Search bar and iTunes will load it for you. Scroll through the main page and the latest releases will be shown front and center, letting you see new music at a glance.

On the right side of the screen you will see Music in big letters, with All Genres under it. Clicking the All Genres link opens a dropdown menu with every main genre you can think of.

The big Music link will open a dropdown menu with the rest of the iTunes store options: Movies, TV Shows, App Store, Books, Podcasts, Audiobooks, and iTunes U. Go through each one and you will see that they all follow the same conventions as the Music page, with charts, top downloads, and new releases.

To purchase new music (or any other media) that interests you, use either the Search bar or browse through the categories to find what you're looking for. When you reach a song or album you'd like, click it to bring up the full information menu for that item.

The window will display all types of information including album price, individual song price, track list, audio previews, release date, ratings, reviews, and similar items. To buy the album (or a single song), click on the price; a prompt window will come up to make sure you really wanted to buy that album, and you can continue by clicking the blue Buy button.

If you already have funds in your iTunes account, or have a card on file, the purchase will be made and the song(s) will begin to automatically download. If you don't have any money in the account, or haven't yet added a payment method, you will be asked to enter that information before the purchase can be made.

After your purchases are fully downloaded, you'll be able to enjoy your new music by clicking on the My Music tab and selecting your latest addition.

iTunes Match

Apple Music is a great service, but if you already have an extensive music library and don't want new music, then iTunes Match might be a solution for you.

iTunes Match is also great if you have a large music library but don't have enough storage on your phone.

Signing up for Match will allow you to store your entire collection on iCloud, including music that you've ripped from CDs and didn't purchase through iTunes. This way you'll be able to stream your entire library from any Apple device connected to iCloud without taking up any storage.

The songs are "matched" by Apple's online music database, so when you are playing the song on your iPhone, for example, it isn't actually the same file that you uploaded or purchased. Rather, it's Apple's version of the song in full 256 Kbps, even if the song you originally uploaded or purchased was of lower audio quality. If the song is not found on Apple's own servers (your cousin's Whitesnake cover band perhaps), it will playback the original file you uploaded, with the original audio quality.

Unfortunately, iTunes Match isn't free. If you'd like to sign up for it, expect to pay $24.99 for a yearly subscription.

APP STORE

The App Store is where you'll be able to download and install many different applications that have been developed specifically for use with a Mac computer. These apps will do everything from add new functionalities and make your life easier, to providing a fun way to waste time and play some games during downtime at work. Keep in mind that for the App Store to be functional, you need to be connected to the Internet.

To be clear, apps purchased on the App Store only run on Macs; if you have two Macs, you can download it on both if you have the same account. But you cannot download them on your iPhone or iPad. So, if you are wondering why a game you downloaded on the iPhone or iPad is not available free on your Mac, that's why. Mac apps are developed using an entirely different framework.

Open the App Store by selecting it either through the Dock or Launchpad. The App Store's home page will greet you, showing you the latest and greatest in the world of apps.

At the top you will see different sections: Featured, Top Charts, Categories, Purchases, and Updates.

The Featured, Top Charts, and Categories tabs will show you apps that can be downloaded, but organized in different ways. Featured will show you Best New Apps, Best New Games, Editor's Choices, and collections of different apps that work great together.

Top Charts shows you the best of the best when it comes to available apps, and is broken down by Top Paid, Top Free, and Top Grossing. On the right side, you can also browse through Top Apps broken down by category, in case you wanted to refine your search.

Categories further breaks down your app hunting into different categories like Business, Education, Reference, Productivity, Medical, Entertainment, and Games.

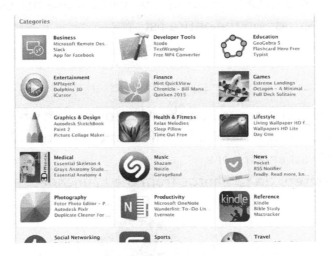

Choosing a category will bring up more selections and the right side will be filled with even more categories. For example, selecting the Business category will bring you to the main Business apps page where the hottest apps are listed. On the right side, smaller categories like Apps for Writers, App Development, or Apps for Designers can be selected. It doesn't matter what category of apps you are currently under; the list remains the same in the right half.

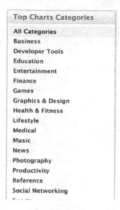

Purchases and Updates are where you can go to view past App Store downloads. The Purchases title can be a bit misleading, because your free apps will also appear here. In the Updates section, you can view which apps need to be updated to the latest version. If you have multiple apps that need updating, you can choose the Update All button and it will go down the entire list.

PHOTOS

Photos has been around on the Mac for quite a while. In OS Catalina, however, it got a bit of a facelift that closer resembles the experience on the iPad and iPhone.

To get started, go to Photos from the Launchpad.

If your Mac is synced to your iPhone, then your photos are synced as well. No need to move them over. If you don't have an iPhone or you have other photos that you'd like to add that weren't taken on an Apple device, then you can go to File > Import.

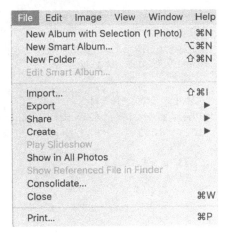

There are a few options to check out in the top menu. The first is the bigger / smaller slider.

This lets you adjust the thumbnail preview size of your photos.

Next to that is the Years / Months / Days / All Photos option, which lets you pick how photos are grouped.

If you have a photo selected, you can click the "i" and see information about the photo (what camera was used, resolution, ISO, file size, and more).

Next to information is the option to share, favorite, rotate, or search for images.

Search is pretty smart—you can search by the names of people or by the location it was taken.

On the left menu, you have the option to view specific photos—photos with people, for example.

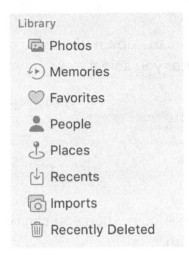

If you go into Memories, you can watch slideshows of past photos (Apple's AI groups these together). To watch the slideshow, right-click (two-finger click) on the memory you want to see.

Under Albums in the left menu, you can right-click to create a new Album.

If you select New Smart Album, then you can create an Album based on a defined filter you select.

Once you create an Album, then you can right-click on any photo and add it to that Album.

When you double-click on any photo, you can edit it. In edit mode, there's an option to auto edit, which adjust the lighting based on what the AI thinks is correct.

There are dozens of basic and advanced editing options.

There are three main sections when doing edits (accessible in the top menu): Adjust (lighting corrections), Filters (pre-defined photo filters), and Crop.

LESSER USED APPS

There are a lot of apps on Mac that you probably see but don't use. Here's a rundown of some of those apps and when you might use them.

TextEdit is Apple's answer to Microsoft's Notepad. This is a simple plain-text editor. It's certainly not fancy, but it's good for jotting down notes.

Stickies is a love it or hate it sort of app. If you're in the love it camp, though, they're still there. Stickies are like Post-it notes for your desktop. Just open the Stickies app from Launchpad and start sticking away!

Make a note of it!

Stickies lets you keep notes (like these) on your desktop. Use a Stickies note to jot down reminders, lists, or other information. You can also use notes to store frequently used text or graphics.

• To close this note, click the close button.

• To collapse this note, double click the title bar.

Your current notes appear when you open Stickies.

Siri

If you've used Siri on the iPhone, iPad or Apple Watch, then you'll be right at home with this feature. Siri is built into the Dock. To use it, just click the Dock icon.

HINT: There's a shortcut key for bringing up Siri: hold the Command key and Spacebar.

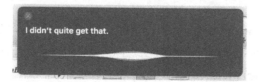

Siri is great for asking general questions, but it also works for doing more involved tasks. Here's a few examples of that:

Drag and Drop Images – Ask Siri to find you photos of something; it will confirm if you want web images or images on your hard drive. It will bring back photos and you can click and drag them into documents, emails, and lots of other things.

Locating Files – Siri works much like the finder…except easier. You can tell Siri to find a specific file, or you can tell Siri to find you all files opened last week, or virtually anything else.

Personal Assistant – Siri is great at doing tasks for you. You can ask Siri to email someone, read text messages, or make an appointment in your calendar. Just ask and see what happens!

If you'd like to change Siri's settings (change the voice from female to male, for example), then go to the Launchpad, open System Preferences, then click Siri.

MacOS Meet iOS

The line between MacOS and iOS gets smaller with each update, and that trend continues with Catalina. The idea is that the apps you use on iOS should look the same on MacOS, so if you know how to use it in one place, you'll know how to use it in the other.

There are four apps in particular: News, Stock, Home, and Voice Memos.

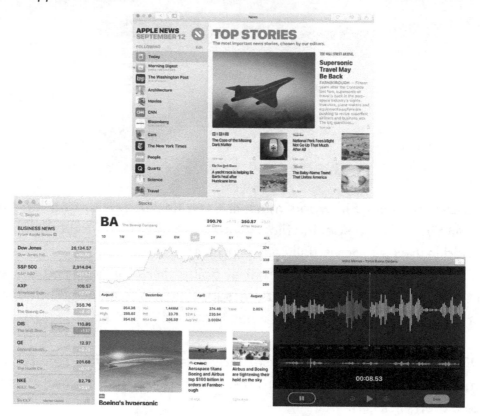

You can access these apps through the sidebar.

Most of these apps will be self-explanatory. Home might be a little new to you, however. Apple has made a strong push on the Home with what it calls HomeKit. Developers can use HomeKit to develop home automation (turn the lights off from your phone sort of thing). If you have a HomePod (the fancy Siri speaker), this is where you would manage that.

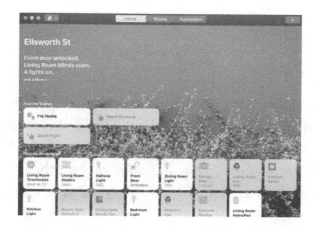

[7]

APPLE SERVICES

This chapter will cover:
- iCloud
- Apple Arcade
- Apple TV+
- Apple Music
- Apple News
- Apple Card

INTRODUCTION

It used to be a few times a year Apple would take the stage and announce something that everyone's head exploded over! The iPhone! The iPad! The Apple Watch! The iPod!

That still happens today, but Apple also is well aware of the reality: most people don't upgrade to new hardware every year. How does a company make money when that happens? In a word: services.

In the past few years (especially in 2019) Apple announced several services—things people would opt into to pay for monthly. It was a way to continue making money even when people were not buying hardware.

For it to work, Apple knew they couldn't just offer a subpar service and expect people to pay because it said Apple. It had to be good. And it is!

iCloud

iCloud is something that Apple doesn't talk a lot about but is perhaps their biggest service. It's estimated that nearly 850 million people use it. The thing about it, however, is many people don't even know they're using it.

What exactly is it? If you are familiar with Google Drive, then the concept is something you probably already understand. It's an online storage locker. But it's more than that. It is a place where you can store files, and it also syncs everything—so if you send a message on your iPhone, it appears on your MacBook and iPad. If you work on a Keynote presentation from your iPad, you can continue where you left off on your iPhone.

What's even better about iCloud is it's affordable. New devices get 5GB for free. From there the price range is as follows (note that these prices may change after printing):

- 50GB: $0.99
- 200GB: $2.99
- 2TB: $9.99

These prices are for everyone in your family. So, if you have five people on your plan, then each person doesn't need their own storage plan. This also means purchases are saved—if one family member buys a book or movie, everyone can access it.

iCloud has become even more powerful as our photo library grows. Photos used to be relatively small, but as cameras have advanced, the size goes up. Most photos on your Mac are several MB big. iCloud means you can keep the newest ones on your phone and put the older ones in the Cloud. It also means you don't have to worry about paying for the phone with the biggest hard drive—in fact, even if you have the biggest hard drive, there's a chance it won't fit all of your photos.

WHERE IS ICLOUD?

If you look at your MacBook, you won't see an iCloud app. That's because there isn't an iCloud app. To see iCloud, point your computer browser to iCloud.com.

Once you sign in, you'll see all the things stored in your Cloud—photos, contacts, notes, files; these are all things you can access across all of your devices.

In addition, you can use iCloud from any computer (even PCs); this is especially helpful if you need to use Find My Mac, which locates not only your computer, but all of your Apple devices—phones, watches, even AirPods.

BACKING UP YOUR COMPUTER WITH ICLOUD

The first thing you should know about iCloud is how to back up your computer with it. This is what you will need to do if you are moving from one Mac to another.

If there's no iCloud app on the computer, then how do you do that? While there is no native app in the traditional sense that you are used to, there are several iCloud settings in System Preferences.

Open the System Preferences; at the top you will see your name and profile picture; click that. That brings up the option to manage iCloud.

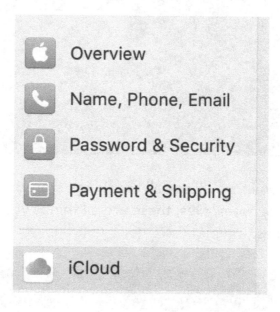

ICLOUD DRIVE

To see your cloud files, open the Finder app; on the left menu, there is an option for the iCloud Drive.

You can use iCloud Drive to create and move folders just like you would in the Finder app.

APPLE ARCADE

Apple Arcade is sort of like Netflix for games. It's $4.99/month (nothing extra for other members of your family—share it with up to five members).

The price gives you access to 100+ games. Unlike some streaming services where you have to play the games online, Apple Arcade lets you download the games to play them offline. You can play them on all your Apple compatible devices: iPhone, iPad, and Apple TV. When you stop playing on your computer, you can start playing where you left off on your TV or iPad.

There are no ads and you can use it with parental controls.

HOW TO SIGN UP

Apple Arcade isn't an app. It's a Service. You only download what you want. You sign up by visiting the App Store and tapping on Arcade.

This brings you to the main Arcade menu where all you have to do is tap Subscribe.

Once you subscribe, you'll see a welcome menu.

The Arcade menu is now replaced by games you can download. Tap Get for any game you want. $4.99 is for everything—not per app.

When you read about the game, be mindful of the app size; if you have limited storage, you want to make sure there's enough room.

The app looks like every other app on your computer. The only difference is the splash screen, which says "Arcade."

CANCELLING ARCADE SUBSCRIPTION

All subscriptions are cancelled the same way on the Mac. With the Mac App Store open, go to the top menu, and select Store > View My Account.

Next, select View Information.

Scroll down until you get to Subscriptions, and select Manage.

Subscriptions: 27 (all time)   Manage

Next, select Edit next to the billing date.

Next billing date: Oct 25, 2019   Edit >

Finally, select Cancel Subscription.

Cancel Subscription   If you cancel now, you can still access your
                             subscription until Oct 25, 2019.

APPLE TV+

Apple has been quietly working on a TV service for quite some time. In 2019, they finally revealed the details. It will be $4.99 a month (free for a year if you buy an iPhone, iPad, Apple Watch, Apple TV, or Mac—note that this may change in the future). It will be available on November 1.

At this printing, there are still some unknowns—notably when certain shows will be released and how many there will be when it launches. What Apple has said is they aren't trying to be like Netflix, having thousands of things to watch. They are focused on quality over quantity.

The shows that are planned to be released on November 1 (again, this could change after this printing):

- The Morning Show – A show about the drama behind the scenes of a morning TV show; it stars Jennifer Aniston, Reese Witherspoon, and Steve Carell.
- Dickinson – A period piece (with a modern flair) about the poet Emily Dickinson starring Haley Steinfeld.
- For All Mankind – An alternative reality drama that imagines what would have happened if the space race had never ended.
- See – An apocalyptic drama starring Jason Momoa about humans trying to survive in a world where nobody can see.
- The Elephant Queen – A documentary about the threat of elephant extinction.
- Snoopy In Space – A new series from Peanuts (i.e. Charlie Brown and company).
- Helpsters – A kids series from the creators of Sesame Street.
- Ghostwriter – A new twist to a 90s kids TV show.

More shows may be out in November, and more shows will definitely come each month—Apple plans to have at least one show / movie out a month. Apple has announced (with no set release dates) that it plans to work with such directors as J. J. Abrams, Steven Spielberg, and M. Night Shyamalan, and actors like Octavia Spencer, Brie Larson, and Jennifer Garner. A new Oprah Winfrey show will also be released.

You'll be able to, of course, watch these shows on Apple TV, iPhones, Macs and iPads.

APPLE MUSIC

Apple Music is Apple's music streaming service.

The question most people wonder is which is better: Spotify or Apple Music? On paper it's hard to tell. They both have the same number of songs, and they both cost the same ($9.99 a month, $5 for students, $14.99 for families).

There really is no clear winner. It all comes down to preference. Spotify has some good features—such as an ad-supported free plan.

One of the standout features of Apple Music is iTunes Match. If you are like me and have a large collection of audio files on your computer, then you'll love iTunes Match. Apple puts those files in the Cloud, and you can stream them on any of your devices. This feature is also available if you don't have Apple Music for $25 a year.

Apple Music also plays well with Apple devices; so, if you are an Apple house (i.e. everything you own, from smart speakers to TV media boxes, has the Apple logo), then Apple Music is probably the best one for you.

Apple is compatible with other smart speakers, but it's built to shine on its own devices.

I won't cover Spotify here, but my advice is to try them both (they both have free trials) and see which interface you prefer.

APPLE MUSIC CRASH COURSE

Before going over where things are in Apple Music, it's worth noting that Apple Music can now be accessed from your web browser (in beta form) here: http://beta.music.apple.com.

It's also worth noting that I have a little girl and don't get to listen to a lot of "adult" music, so the examples here are going to show a lot of kid's music!

The main navigation on Apple Music is on the side menu:

- For You
- Browse
- Radio

Apple Music

♥ For You

🎵 Browse

((•)) Radio

There's also a Library below this of what you have downloaded.

Library

🕐 Recently Added

🎤 Artists

🎵 Albums

🎵 Songs

Music Videos

▢ TV & Movies

LIBRARY

When you create playlists or download songs or albums, this is where you will go to find them.

You can change the categories that show up in this first list by tapping on Edit, then checking off the categories you want. Make sure to hit Done to save your changes.

FOR YOU

As you play music, Apple Music starts to get to know you more and more; it makes recommendations based on what you are playing.

In For You, you can get a mix of all these songs and see other recommendations.

In addition to different styles of music, it also has friends' recommendations so you can discover new music based on what your friends are listening to.

BROWSE

Not digging those recommendations? You can also browse genres in the Browse menu. In addition to different genre categories, you can see what music is new and what music is popular.

RADIO

Radio is Apple's version of AM/FM; the main radio station is Beats One. There are on-air DJs and everything you'd expect from a radio station.

While Beats One is Apple's flagship station, it's not its only station. You can scroll down and tap on Radio Stations under More to explore and see several other stations based on music styles (i.e. country, alternative, rock, etc.). Under this menu, you'll also find a handful of talk stations covering news and sports. Don't expect to find the opinionated talk radio you may listen to on regular radio—it's pretty controversy-free.

SEARCH

The last option is the search menu, which is pretty self-explanatory. Type in what you want to find (i.e. artist, album, genre, etc.).

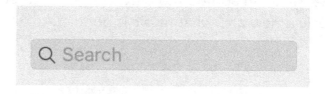

LISTENING TO MUSIC AND CREATING A PLAYLIST

You can access the music you are currently listening to from the top of your screen.

Right-clicking (two-finger clicking) on the album on this brings up several options. One is to take you to the album, which shows a full screen view.

Clicking on the chat-like button will show you the text from what's playing.

To the left of that is the option to select where you want to play the music. For example, if you have a HomePod and you want to listen wirelessly to the music from that device, you can change it here.

The option on the far right shows the next song(s) in the playlist.

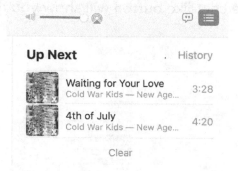

If you want to add a song to a playlist, then right-click the song and select the playlist (or create one).

At any point, you can tap the artist's name to see all of their music.

In addition to seeing information about the band, their popular songs, and their albums, you can get a playlist of their essential songs or a playlist of bands that they have influenced.

Artist Playlists

If you scroll to the bottom, you can also see Similar Artists, which is a great way to discover new bands that are like the ones you are currently listening to.

Tips for Getting the Most Out of Apple Music

Heart It

Like what you're hearing? Heart it! Hate it? Dislike it. Apple gets to know you by what you listen to, but it improves the accuracy when you tell it what you think of a song you are really into…or really hate.

Download Music

If you don't want to rely on wi-fi when you are on the go, make sure and tap the cloud on your music to download the music locally to your phone. If you don't see a cloud, add it to your library by tapping the plus, which should change it to a cloud.

Hey Siri

Siri knows music! Say "Hey Siri" and say what you want to listen to, and the AI will get to work.

APPLE NEWS

In 2012, a little app with big ambitions called Next (it was later changed to Texture) disrupted the magazine industry by creating the Netflix of magazines. For one low price, you could read hundreds of magazines (and their back issues, too). They weren't small indie magazines—they were the big ones: People, Time, Wired, and more.

Apple took notice, and, in 2018, they acquired the company. The writing was on the wall: Apple wanted to get into print services.

In 2019, it was announced that Texture would close because Apple would release a new service called News+. News+ does everything that Texture did, but also combines newspapers (Los Angeles Times and The Wall Street Journal).

There is a free version of the service that curates news for you; the paid version that carries the magazine subscriptions is $9.99. (You can have five family members on your plan.)

What really makes Apple News stand out is it's curated for you and your tastes. If you have other family members on your plan, it will be curated for them as well—it's based on the user's tastes, so if you have a family member into entertainment news and you are into game news, you won't see their interests—only yours.

APPLE NEWS CRASH COURSE

To get started, open the News app from your Launchpad.

The UI for the app is pretty simple—and is almost identical on iPhone and iPad, so there's limited to no learning curve if you already use it on one of those.

~ Today—This is where you'll find your curated news.

News+—Where you'll find magazines.

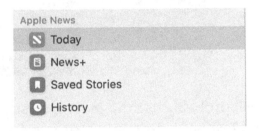

TODAY

The Today menu gives you all your news (starting with the top news / breaking news) in a scrolling format.

Top Stories

The New York Times
Turkey launches Syria attack, targeting militia backed by U.S.

The Washington Post
Biden says Trump should be impeached as president calls for end of inquiry

Right-click on any story and get several options.

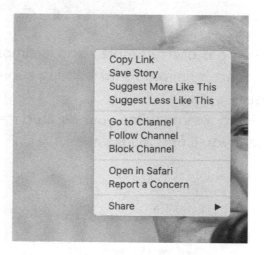

The one you will probably use the most is to suggest more / less like this; these two options help Apple News understand what you are into and will over time start to personalize stories based on your preferences.

Typically, "report" in a news app means you find it somehow inappropriate in nature; that's true here, but there are other reasons to report it—such as, it's dated wrong, it's in the wrong category, it's a broken link, or something else.

As you scroll down, you start seeing different categories (Trending Stories in the example below); when you tap the three dots with a circle, you'll get an option to block it, so it won't show in your feed any longer.

Trending Stories

When you tap to read a story, there are only a few options.

To make the text larger or smaller, use the view option in the menu above and zoom in or out.

One criticism of Apple News by some has been its UI; when Apple announced the service along with its partnership with the Los Angeles Times and Wall Street Journal, many expected a format similar to what you have seen with the magazines section—a full newspaper-type lay-out.

Worse, many didn't even know how to find the newspaper. And if they did find it, they couldn't search for stories. While the app is pretty resourceful, this is still an early product and some of the features you want might not be there yet.

That said, you can "kind of" read the Los Angeles Times (or any newspaper in Apple News) in a more traditional way. First, find an article in your feed from the publication you want to see more from, and then click the publication's name at the top of the story.

Los Angeles Times

This will bring up the publication along with all the topics from that publication.

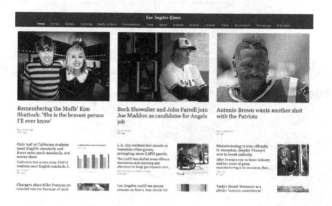

If you want to search for a particular story or publication, then use the search box in the upper right corner.

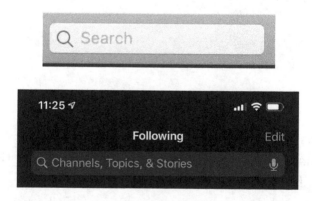

NEWS+

The last section to cover is News+; this is where you'll find all the magazines you love.

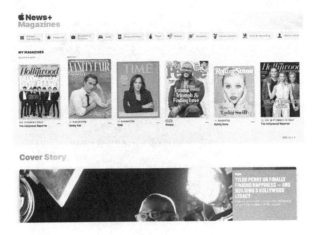

The format is similar to the Today screen; magazines you read are at the top; below that are stories pulled from several different magazines that the app thinks you'll be interested in.

When you read articles from the list, it opens in the actual magazine and looks a little different from articles in the Today area.

Anytime you want to read more from a magazine (or see back issues) just click the logo from an article you are reading.

That brings up a list of all the issues you can read as well as some of the latest stories from the magazine.

Right-clicking on the magazine cover brings up several options—including the option to Follow the channel, which lets you know when new issues are available.

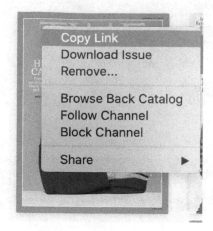

To browse all the magazines available, select Browse the Catalog from the main screen (or browse by a category that you are interested in).

This brings up a list of all the magazines you can read (at this writing, there are around 300).

APPLE CARD

One of Apple's most talked about new products is Apple Card. Apple Card is a credit card that, at first glance, doesn't differ from most credit cards. It may not have the best rewards (1% to 3% cash back depending on your purchase) or best interest rate, but that doesn't mean it's not disrupting the industry; it's definitely something you should consider getting.

On the surface, the advantage of Apple Card is receiving your rewards the next day—not waiting for them. That's nice. But where it excels is in security and how it helps you keep track of purchases.

Apple Card can be added to a Mac, but Macs aren't really made to make purchases at checkout counters—most people won't get to a checkout stand and whip out a MacBook to pay. For this reason and more, the Mac doesn't have a native Wallet app.

You will find the option to add, manage, and, in the case of the Apple Card, pay bills in the System Preferences. Storing your card on your iPad or iPhone will let you pay at online retailers.

Because Apple Card is best experienced on an iPhone, I'm going to walk through how to do it on the iPhone below.

Once you add it on the iPhone, then go to System Preferences on your Mac to manage it.

GETTING YOUR CARD

Getting an Apple Card will probably be the easiest credit card sign up you have ever experienced in your life. To get started, go to the Wallet app on your iPhone.

When the app opens, click the '+' button and follow the application. It will just ask you a series of questions and then tell you if you are approved.

If you're approved, your card will appear in your Wallet app with other cards.

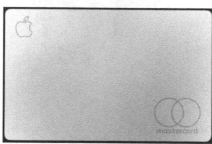

WHEN THERE IS NO APPLE PAY

Once you are approved for the card, you can start using it! There's no need to wait for the card—in fact the rewards are better if you don't use the card!

But sometimes you need a card. Not everyone accepts Apple Pay, after all. Fortunately, you can request a card.

You'll probably be surprised by the card. It's thick. Like really thick. Like probably the thickest card in your wallet! You can't even bend it. It doesn't feel like a plastic card. It feels like metal. That's because it's made of metal. It's not heavy at all, fortunately.

It takes about a week to arrive, and activating it is probably going to impress you. There's no number to call. No number to input on a website. None of that stuff.

It comes in a stylish envelope; when you lift the flap of the envelope and put it next to the bottom of your iPhone, it will recognize the card and start the activation process. It looks a bit like the screen below—the card in the illustration was already activated, so the steps are no longer there. The whole process is quick, stylish, and seamless—everything you'd expect from Apple.

Many people think they have to wait for their card to use it online where Apple Pay isn't accepted. That's not true. You just need the credit card number. I know, I know—there is no credit card number! That's where you are wrong. There's no visible number, but there is a number.

To see it, tap the card in your Wallet app, and then tap the three little dots near the top.

This opens up your account information where you can see your credit limit, interest rate, make payments, and contact support. One of the options is "Card Information."

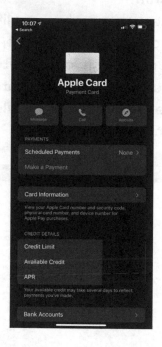

Here you'll be able to see your card number, expiration, and security code. Worried someone has your number? Just request a new number.

Requesting a new number doesn't affect your physical card. If someone steals your physical card, then make sure you deactivate that, and request a new card. How do you do that? Hit the back arrow to go back to your account menu. Scroll down to Request Replacement Card. This will suspend your account to stop any future transactions and a new card will be sent.

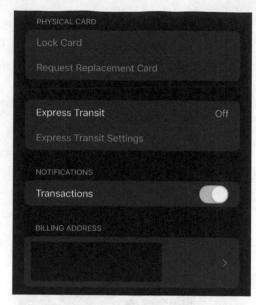

What if you want to remove the card? Go back a screen, and then go to the bottom of the screen and tap Remove This Card (remember, however, that this won't close out your account).

SEEING CARD ACTIVITY

When you tap your card from the Wallet app, you can see all your activity, such as balance, when the payment is due, and recent transactions.

Not sure what a transaction is? Tap on it and you'll get more information about the store, and, in many cases, see a map of where it was purchased. This is helpful when tracking down mystery payments which appear on other credit cards with weird names that don't make any sense and seem more like codes than businesses.

If you tap on Monthly Activity from the previous screen, you can see the categories in which you are spending money. You can also see your rewards.

The big question on your mind might be how you spend those rewards. The rewards money is on a separate card called a Cash Card that you can access from your Wallet app. You can spend the money by using it anywhere that takes Apple Pay, or you can transfer the money straight to your bank account. You can also use the Cash Card to text money to friends.

MAKING PAYMENTS AND SEEING STATEMENTS

To make a payment to your card, go to your main card page and tap the Payment Due box. This brings up your payment information. Interest is very transparent on Apple Card. See those dots on the circle? Tap the check mark and drag it to one of those dots; this tells you what your interest charge would be by only making a portion of the payment. Drag to the area you want to pay and then select Pay Now (or Pay Later to schedule the payment). If you don't have your bank account set up, then you'll have to do that at this point—you'll need your bank account number and routing information.

To see your credit card statement, tap Total Balance from the main menu. Go to the bottom and select the statement you want to see.

This brings up a brief, high-level, digital statement.

If you want to see your full statement—the long paper one you'd typically get in the mail from other credit cards—then tap Download PDF Statement.

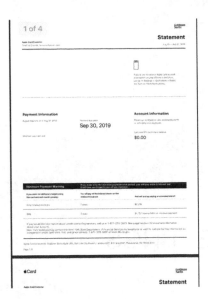

[8]
SYSTEM SETTINGS

This chapter will cover:
- System preferences
- Adding social networking and other accounts
- Controlling sound
- User groups
- Screenshots
- Photo continuity
- Accessibility
- Privacy / security

So now you know the basics; you should be able to work your way around the desktop with ease and use all the basic programs comfortably. But it still doesn't feel quite...you. It still has all the default settings, colors, gestures, and backgrounds. Sure it's a cool computer, but now let's make it feel like your computer.

SYSTEM PREFERENCES

All of the main settings are accessed in System Preferences which is essentially the Mac equivalent of Control Panel on a Windows computer. So to get started, let's get to System Preferences by clicking Launchpad, then clicking the System Preferences icon.

You can also get there by clicking on the Apple in the upper left corner of the menu and clicking System Preferences.

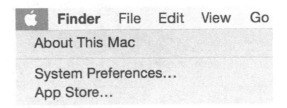

Once the app opens, you'll see there are lots of things that you can configure.

General

Let's get started with the first option: General. Under General, you can:

- Change the appearance of the main buttons, windows, and menus by selecting either Blue or Graphite.
- Choose the highlight color.

- Change the top menu bar and Dock to dark colors. This option works well with dark wallpapers.
- Set scroll bars to display automatically based on mouse or Track-pad, only when scrolling, or always on.
- Select the default web browser.
- Here is where you can allow Handoff to work between your Mac and iCloud devices (some older Macs don't support this feature).

At any time, you can get back to the main System Preferences page by clicking on the button with 12 tiny squares. You can also hit the Back button, but if you are several menus in, you may have to hit the Back button several times.

Desktop & Screen Saver

The Desktop & Screen Saver section will help you change perhaps the most visually noticeable thing on your Mac—the desktop wallpaper. Along the left sidebar you will see several different dropdown options: Apple, iPhoto, and Folders.

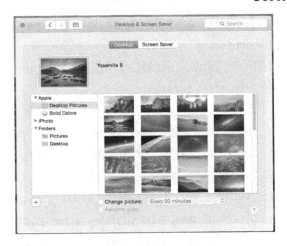

At the bottom, you will be able to change the picture every so often, and you can choose how often you'd like a new image to refresh. The images that show up in the right-hand window will be the ones that get scrolled through during refreshes.

To change your desktop wallpaper to one of the great-looking images provided by Apple, or if you just want to browse the available choices, click on the Apple name. A bunch of colorful, high-resolution images will populate the right-hand side, and you can scroll through the list to find something you like. Clicking on an image will change your wallpaper to that particular selection. If you're a plain Jane and prefer to keep things really simple, you can also select Solid Colors to find an array of potentially yawn-inducing plain wallpapers.

Selecting iPhoto will let you scroll through your photos, allowing you to select a cherished memory as your wallpaper.

The Folders option will let you choose between added folders where more image files might be lying in wait. If you save lots of images to your desktop, you might want to add the Desktop folder here so you can include those images as would-be wallpapers.

Adding and Removing Folders
1. To add new folders and image collections, click on the '+' button located at the bottom of the left sidebar.
2. When the window comes up, search for the folder that you'd like to add.

3. Once you find the desired folder, click the blue Choose button to confirm the changes.
4. To remove a folder, highlight the folder that you'd like deleted and then click the '–' button to remove it.

Screen Saver

To set one up, click on the Screen Saver button at the top of the Desktop & Screen Saver window.

The left sidebar will have more options than you probably need when it comes to different ways to display your pictures. Some great ones you will probably like are Shuffling Tiles, Vintage Prints, and Classic.

On the right side you can see a preview of what your screen saver will look like. In this part of the window you can also select a source: National Geographic, Aerial, Cosmos, Nature Patterns, and Choose Folder if you have a particular folder of images you'd like to use. If you'd like to shuffle the order in which images appear, check the box next to Shuffle slide order.

At the very bottom of the window you can choose the length of time before the screen saver starts. You'll also be able to pick if you'd like to display the clock or not.

Dock

There isn't a lot you can do to the Dock and most of these settings are self-explanatory. For the most part the settings just make things a little more...animated. Magnification, for example, makes an app icon larger when you hover your mouse over it.

One option I will point out, however, is the option to automatically hide and show Dock; all of these settings are a matter of taste; I personally choose to hide the Dock for two reasons: one, it gives you more screen space, and two, it lets you use the Dock while you are in a full screen app.

Mission Control

Mission Control is where you can set different parts of your screen to do different things. What do I mean by that? For example, you can set up a shortcut so that every time you move your mouse to the far upper right corner, your desktop is revealed. You can also set up shortcut keys on your keyboard. Mission Control is really about helping you make simple tasks quick.

Social Networking, Mail, Contacts and Calendars

When you use Twitter, Facebook and other apps, you may be used to just going to a website. On a Mac, you can add them into your computer's information, so you don't need to login; this also lets you get notification pop ups when you have new messages, likes, etc.

Adding Accounts

To add accounts, go to System Preferences on your Dock (the gears icon) and select Internet Accounts. From here, you can add accounts that haven't already been migrated, including iCloud, Exchange, Google, Twitter, Facebook, LinkedIn, Yahoo!, AOL, Vimeo and Flickr. Adding accounts here will start populating Catalina's native Mail, Contacts, Reminders and Calendar apps, and add options to your Share button.

Note: You can also add accounts within the Mail, Contacts, Calendars, and Reminders apps by opening each app and clicking File > Add Account.

Twitter, Facebook, LinkedIn, Vimeo and Flickr

Catalina OS supports deep Twitter, Facebook, LinkedIn, Flickr and Vimeo integration. To get started, simply sign in to your account(s) from System Preferences > Internet Accounts. Select Twitter, Facebook, LinkedIn, Flickr, or Vimeo, and then enter your username and password. From now on, you'll be able to use that account with the Share button throughout Catalina and receive notifications in your Notifications Center.

IMG_0030.jpg

SOUND

As the name implies, the Sound menu is where all changes related to sound effects and sound in general can be modified. There are three tabs that you can switch between.

Sound Effects

The Sound Effects tab is where you can select an alert sound from the many different built-in options. By default, the following dropdown menu should be set to Selected sound output device to play the chosen sound effects through your standard speakers.

The next two checkboxes let you turn sound effects on or off for the user interface, and for volume control.

Lastly, you'll be able to adjust the output volume of your speakers. This will affect the loudness of everything from sound effects to music that's currently being played through the computer.

Input & Output

The input and output tabs are both very similar. Each will let you change the device for sound input or output (speakers or microphones), as well as adjust sound settings. In the output tab, you can adjust the slider to move the balance left or right, and in input, you can change the microphone's input volume and enable or disable the built-in noise reduction feature in case you frequently use your Mac's microphone in busy cafes.

USERS & GROUPS

If your Mac is for family use and a couple of people will be using it, then this setting will come in handy.

Along the left sidebar all existing users and groups (if you have any) will be laid out for you. To make a change to an existing user, first you need to choose the "Click the lock" icon and unlock it; unlocking lets you change settings to the user. You will also be asked for your password at this time—this is all a safety measure to ensure that if you accidentally left your computer unattended, someone couldn't come along and lock you out of your own machine.

Below are a few things you'll be able to do with each user. Depending on the type of user it is (admin, guest, child, etc.), some of the settings won't be available.

- Selecting the admin user account will let you change the login password, open up the Contacts card and enable parental controls. Clicking the Login Items will allow you to change the applications that start running automatically each time you log in. There has to be at least one admin user.

- Any other created users that you make will have options to enable parental controls, change password, or turn that account into another administrator account that has full control of the Mac.

- By default, you will see a guest user set up. If it's selected, you can choose to disable the guest user from being available as a login option. You can also set parental controls and allow guest access to your shared folders. If you do choose to keep the guest user, keep in mind that there will be no password required, and all information and files created during that session will be deleted upon logging out.

- At the bottom of the left sidebar there is another option, called Login Options. This is where you'll find different options such as automatic login, show password hints, and show the Sleep, Shut Down, and Restart buttons. You can also display your full name or user name at the top right of the menu bar by checking the box next to Show fast user switching menu and making a selection.

Create New Users

So you know how to manage the primary user, but what about creating additional users? That's pretty simple. Just follow these steps (and make sure you have already hit that lock button to unlock the option).

1. Click on the '+' button.
2. From the New Account dropdown menu, choose from the following options: Administrator, Standard, Managed with Parental Controls, or Sharing Only.

3. Fill in the Full Name and Account Name fields. These don't have to be real names. Mickey Mouse can have a user name if you want.

4. You can choose to have the new user log in using an existing iCloud account and password, or create a whole new password.

5. If you selected Use iCloud Password, you will be prompted to enter the associated iCloud ID.

6. If you instead choose to opt for a newly-created password, you will be asked to enter it twice to verify it.

7. Once finished, click the blue Create User button. If you chose to use an iCloud ID, you will be asked to enter the password. If you made a new password, you don't need to do anything else.

Removing Existing Users

Just because you added a user, that doesn't mean they're there forever. You can delete them at any time. But remember, deleting them deletes all the settings they've set up—so if you create that user again, everything will be gone.

1. To remove current users, select the user that you'd like to delete.

2. With that user highlighted, click on the '–' button.

3. A prompt will appear asking if you are really sure you'd like to remove the user from the computer.

4. You can also choose from one of three radio buttons: save the home folder, leave the home folder alone, or delete the home folder.
5. Once you've made a decision, click the blue Delete User button to confirm your choice and make the changes happen.

Creating Groups

If the computer is being used in a place where there are dozens of users (a classroom or library, perhaps), then creating a group would be a good option for you.

1. At the bottom of the left sidebar, click the '+' button.
2. From the New dropdown menu, select Group
3. In the Full Name field, create and enter a name for your group.
4. Click the blue Create Group button to confirm.
5. The new group will be created, and you will be able to check boxes next to each existing user to designate who will be a part of this group. If you have existing groups, you can also select entire groups to be a part of yet another group.

SNAP THIS

Screenshots on MacOS have always been pretty simple and straightforward. Shift-Command-3 to take a screenshot of your entire screen and Shift-Command-4 to take a screenshot of a specific area of your screen.

These commands still work, but Apple took it up a notch and allows you to edit the screenshot—if you've taken screenshots on iOS, then the experience is probably familiar to you.

As soon as you take a screenshot, you'll see options for what you can do next in a small popup at the bottom right of your screen. These options will take you to a Markup window where you can add annotations, shapes, text, and more.

In addition to these options, MacOS has added a new command: Shift-Command-5. This opens up a screenshot interface with several options such as capture entire screen, selected window, or a selected portion. The last two options are new: record the entire screen or record a portion of it.

CONTINUE THAT PHOTO WHERE YOU LEFT OFF

One thing Apple has done really well with their devices is continuity—the idea of stopping on one device and picking up where you left off on another. For example, you could stop a movie in the living room on Apple TV and continue watching it on your Apple TV in the bedroom. Or you could get a text on your Apple Watch and reply on your phone. It's all very intuitive and just works.

This concept of using on one device and picking up on another now extends to the camera. With OS Catalina, you can take a picture on your iPhone or iPad and have it automatically sent to your Mac and into the photo editing app of your desire.

If the Mac app supports the feature, then you'll see it under Edit in the menu area; there will be a new option that says "Insert from Your iPhone or iPad" with the option to Take Photo or Scan Documents.

Once you snap the photo on your phone or tablet, it will automatically appear in the document.

ACCESSIBILITY

Accessibility helps you adjust the computer if you have any kind of impairment or disability. It lets you change things like making the display larger, having a voiceover that describes what's on your screen, and put captions on videos when available.

To open Accessibility, click System Settings and Accessibility. On the left side of the box that comes up will be all the various things you can change. Clicking on each one will create more options.

Vision

Under Display, you can make the screen grayscale, invert colors, decrease the contrast, etc. Zoom allows you to create a zoom effect over smaller areas of the screen when you hit a keyboard shortcut. VoiceOver reads back any text that's on the screen.

Media

The Media section includes a few different settings for audio and video playback. Click on Descriptions to enable spoken descriptions for videos.

Captions will apply subtitles and captions to videos.

Hearing

The Sound tab provides options for the hearing disabled. You can choose to set up a visual flash of the screen each time an alert sound is played, and also decide if you'd like to play stereo audio as mono instead.

Interacting

Keyboard includes settings for Sticky Keys and Slow Keys. Sticky Keys allows certain buttons to remain activated without you having to hold down the key. For example, if you have Sticky Keys turned on and want to copy some text, instead of holding down Command-C at the same time, you could press the Command button first, followed by the C key. When enabled, you'll hear a lock sound, and any time you use a modifier key like Command, a large icon will appear in the top right corner of the screen indicating that a Sticky Key combination has been started. Slow Keys increases the amount of time between a button press and activation, so if you press Enter, it will take a little longer to actually process.

Mouse & Trackpad features settings like Mouse Keys, which lets you move the mouse around using the number pad on your keyboard, double-click speed, and the option to ignore the built-in Trackpad (on MacBooks) if there is a separate mouse or Trackpad connected to the computer.

Switch Control requires you to enter your administrator password before making any changes, because it's a powerful function that allows you to control the computer using one or more switches that you designate. You can also modify other settings like what to do while navigating, determine pointer precision, and change the size for the Switch Control cursor.

The Dictation tab does exactly what it sounds like—it lets you dictate commands and write or edit text using only your voice. To enable dictation, you first need to click on the bottom button that says Open Dictation & Speech Preferences and selecting the On radio button.

Voice Control

Voice Control lets you control your computer with your voice.

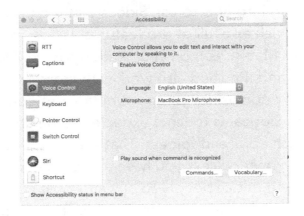

SIDECAR

What's Sidecar? It's basically using your iPad as a second screen alongside your Mac.

Using your iPad as a second Mac screen is nothing new. Popular apps such as Duet have been doing this successfully for years.

Apple has finally taken note and decided to release a feature called Sidecar that lets you wirelessly use your iPad as a secondary Mac screen; it's just like using AirPlay on your phone to show YouTube on your TV. So long apps like Duet, right? Not exactly.

Before moving into how to use Sidecar, let me first mention what Sidecar is not: a rich app full of pro features. It does one thing very well: shows your Mac screen on your iPad. Apps like Duet are compatible with iPhone and iPad and also work with cross OSes—so you can also show your Windows device on your iPad. But personally, one thing I find lacking on Sidecar is touch. I expected to be able to tap the iPad screen and launch apps and folders. That wasn't the case. It was for display purposes only...unless you have an Apple Pencil. Sidecar feels like it was made to entice people to buy an Apple Pencil. With an Apple Pencil, touch suddenly becomes possible. There's probably a good reason for this—the Apple Pencil is more precise and has more gestures than your finger.

So now that you know a little about what it isn't, let's look at how it works.

First, make sure your MacBook (yes, this is only compatible with MacBooks—sorry Windows users) is up-to-date with the latest OS (Catalina).

Second, make sure your iPad is turned on, in standby mode, and on the same Wi-Fi network (if not, you won't see the next step).

Third, go to the menu in the upper right side of your MacBook and click the rectangular box for AirPlay.

That's it! Kind of. Your MacBook should now be showing on your iPad. It will look a little like this:

So what do I mean "kind of"? There are still a few more settings you should know about. Click that AirPlay box in the right corner again and you'll see even more options.

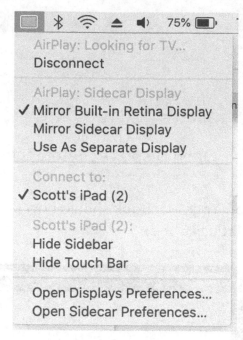

What are all these options? Use As Separate Display (vs the two Mirror options) turns your iPad into a second screen—so you can have another Mac app running on your display instead of just showing whatever is on your MacBook. The two Hide options get rid of the boxes you see on your iPad to make it a bit more full screen.

Finally, Open Sidecar Preferences will give you a few additional options. You can, for example, pick to show the menu bar on the right instead of left.

You can disconnect from Sidecar by either tapping on the box with the line through it on your iPad or going to the AirPlay button on your Mac and disconnecting.

PRIVACY AND SECURITY

If your computer is in a place where other people can get to it, or if you are just generally concerned about your privacy being violated, then head on over to Privacy and Security in the System Preferences.

Creating Strong Passwords

Strong passwords are the first line of defense against potential hackers (or smart children!); a strong password is not something like "password"; a strong password has letters, numbers and even symbols in it. It could be something like this: "@mY_MACb00k."

You can use the Password Assistant to test how strong your password is.

When Keychain loads, you will be able to view the entire list of accounts that are already synced to Keychain. If you would like to change the password for an account that already exists, find the account and double-click on it. If not, click on the '+' button at the bottom to add a new account.

When the new window comes up, take a look at the bottom. There will be a field for password, and at the right of it will be a small key icon. Click the key icon to open up Password Assistant.

From Type you can select Manual (create your own), Memorable, Letters & Numbers, Numbers Only, Random, and FIPS-181 compliant.

Suggestions will automatically populate, and you can scroll through several different suggestions by using the dropdown menu.

Adjust the length slider to make the password longer or shorter. Any password you create will meet at least these requirements to be considered fair.

As you generate a password, the quality indicator will change to show you how safe and complex a given password is.

Firewall

Another line of defense you can add is a firewall, which protects you from unwanted connections to potentially malicious software applications, websites, or files.

To enable the firewall that comes with your Mac, go to System Preferences > Security & Privacy and select the Firewall tab. Before you can make any changes, click on the lock icon in the bottom left corner and enter your administrator password to continue.

Find My Mac

Just like your iPhone or iPad, Mac comes with a handy feature called "Find My Mac" which lets you find your computer if someone steals it or you just misplace it; you can also wipe its hard drive clean remotely.

To enable Find My Mac, go to System Preferences > iCloud and check the box next to Find My Mac. Your location services must also be turned on, so go to System Preferences > Security & Privacy > Privacy > Location Services and make sure Enable Location Services is checked on.

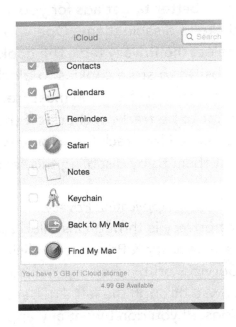

To track your computer, you can log into any computer and visit iCloud.com, enter your iCloud login information, and click on Find My Mac. As long as the Mac is awake and connected to the Internet through Wi-Fi or Ethernet, you will be able to play a loud sound, lock it, or completely erase it so your private information is removed.

Privacy

Apple knows people worry about privacy; they have lots built in to help you control what can (and can't) be seen.

Internet Privacy

If you'd like to clear your search and browsing history, there are two ways to do it: either by clicking on Safari > Clear History and Website Data or History > Clear History and Website Data. Both can be found on the top menu bar. When the window comes up, you will be able to choose how far back you want the clearing to reach. Once you make a selection just press the Clear History button to make the changes final.

Cookies allow websites to store data and track certain things, like what other websites you visit during your Internet session, or what kind of products you tend to look at the most. This information is mostly used by advertisers to better target ads for you, but the option is always there if you'd like to disable them. Open up Safari, go to Safari > Preferences, then select the Privacy tab. The cookie options range from allowing all websites to store cookies to blocking all websites. You can also allow cookies only from the most frequently visited websites. If you prefer not to be tracked, check off the box at the bottom that says Ask Websites To Not Track Me. Some websites will not function as you may want them to by disabling this feature.

Application Privacy

The other part of privacy is through installed applications. Go to System Preferences > Security & Privacy and click the Privacy tab. You can shut Location Services off by checking the box next to Enable Location Services. Browse through the left sidebar and you'll be able to customize permissions. If you don't want any apps to access your contacts or calendars, here is where you can block some or all programs from that information.

Screen Time

Screen Time might be something you are familiar with. It's been on iPads and iPhones for a while. It comes to MacOS with the Catalina update. What is it? It's a productivity setting that lets you restrict how long you can use certain apps (games for instance). It's highly customizable, so you can set one app like Word to have zero restrictions, but another one like Internet to have limits.

Screen Time isn't an app in the traditional sense; it's an app within your system settings. To use it, go to System Preferences, then click Screen Time.

This launches a new window that tells you how much time you've been on your computer.

You can set up a passcode by clicking on options at the bottom of the window.

App Limits is where you can start restricting certain apps. Click the '+' in this section.

From here select the app (or kinds of apps) that you want to limit.

At the bottom, you can say how much time you want to set the limit to.

Under Always Allow, you can select apps that have no restrictions.

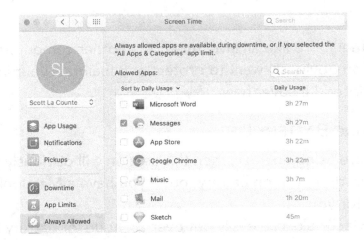

196 | *Apple For Seniors*

[9]

Keep It running Smoothly

This chapter will cover:
- Preserving battery life
- iCloud
- Time Machine
- Software updates

Macs feel more like an investment than other computers; with that in mind, you obviously want to protect and maintain your investment. In this chapter, I'll cover how.

Preserving Battery Life

If you are using an iMac, then this section will obviously not apply since iMacs don't run on battery, but if you have a MacBook, then this section is for you.

Most MacBooks can easily get over six hours of battery life, but there are things you can do to get even more.

- Go to System Preferences > Energy Saver and under the Battery tab, choose to put hard disks to sleep whenever possible, and dim the display slightly while on battery power. You don't want to set it too low, or you'll find it going to sleep when you are reading or doing a task that doesn't require movement.

- Keep the screen only as bright as you need to clearly see the screen. The F1 key will minimize the brightness and F2 will make it bright again. If you are at the beach then you will want the brightest, of course; but if you are in a dark room do you really need full brightness? Probably not.
- The keyboard also has brightness that can be adjusted with F5 and F6 on your keyboard. Backlight on the keyboard really helps in a lowlight setting, but when it's broad daylight, you really don't need it—even at the brightest, you probably would not even be able to tell that it's on.
- When you run websites with Flash, you are killing your battery. Be cautious of what you are using—especially if you are low on battery.

ICLOUD

iCloud lets you store things like photos and videos online. It's kind of like Google Drive or Dropbox. Best of all you get 5GB for free. Lots of cloud-based storage sites give you more storage than Apple—so why use it?

- You'll be able to back up your contacts so they are synced perfectly across your Mac, iPhone, iPad, and iPod. Make a change in a contact card or add a new contact, and the change or addition will be reflected across all of your synced iCloud devices.
- Media files purchased through the iTunes Store won't count against your storage.
- It makes files available across all of your Mac devices.

If you haven't set up an iCloud account, you can create one by going to System Preferences > iCloud and following the on-screen instructions. Once you're finished, you'll be able to select what kind of data you'd like synced through iCloud: Photos, Mail, Contacts, Calendars, Safari, Notes, Keychain, and more. At the bottom you will notice a bar that indicates how much storage has been used up, and how much available storage you have left.

If you want more storage, you can pay extra. The following are the rates as of this writing:

198 | *Apple For Seniors*

- 20 GB for $0.99 a month
- 200 GB for $3.99 a month
- 500 GB for $9.99 a month
- 1 TB for $19.99 a month

If you decide to change your mind and don't need the extra storage plans, Apple gives you 15 days to contact them and ask for a refund.

Time Machine

Everyone worries about losing their data; Apple helps you out with one of their most powerful behind-the-scenes apps: Time Machine.

Time Machine will back up all of your files, applications, and settings with minimal configuration or headache. In the case of a catastrophic event such as hard drive failure, having a Time Machine backup can allow you to quickly recover all of your data and applications, and even all of your settings (such as your desktop background and even the specific location of icons on your desktop).

You will need to buy an external USB or Thunderbolt hard drive. It is recommended to buy a drive that is larger than the current used space on your computer. For example, if you have used 100 gigabytes of space on your computer's hard drive, you should buy at least a 120-gigabyte hard drive.

You can also purchase an additional Time Machine Airport Capsule that does all of this wirelessly.

To get started, plug the hard drive into your computer and Time Machine will start automatically. It will ask you if you would like to use the drive as a Time Machine Backup Disk. Choose Use as Backup Disk.

If Time Machine does not start automatically, go to Finder > Applications > Machine, and click Choose Backup Disk. Select your new hard drive.

After you specify the drive to use as a backup, Time Machine will automatically begin backing up your data.

SOFTWARE UPDATES

If you want your computer running smoothly then make sure you update regularly; updates are free and come once every couple of months. They fix minor bugs and sometimes add things to correct vulnerabilities that might make your computer open to viruses.

MacOS X, by default, will prompt you when updates are available, and you need only to click "Update" and enter your password in order to run the updates. Sometimes, in the case of major updates, you will need to restart your computer to complete the update. You can click Not now if you would like to delay the updates until a more convenient time.

[10]

iWORK FOR MAC

This chapter will cover:
- The iWork Crash Course

HOW TO GET PAGES

Depending on how you acquired your Mac, you may or may not have Pages already. Getting it is easy. And even better: getting it is free! (you can see if you have it by going into the Launchpad from the dock and searching for Pages).

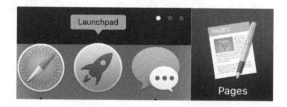

There's one catch: not all Macs are supported. But most are. MacOS 10.14 is required to run Pages, which means you must have one of the following computers:
- MacBook: Early 2015 or newer
- MacBook Air: Mid 2012 or newer
- MacBook Pro: Mid 2012 or newer
- Mac Mini: Late 2012 or newer
- iMac: Late 2012 or newer

- iMac Pro
- Mac Pro: Late 2013 or newer; Mid 2010 or Mid 2012 models require a Metal-capable GPU

As long as you have one of those, then you can go to the App Store (it's in your Launchpad). Pages is a digital download only—you cannot obtain a physical copy of it. The download is a few hundred MB.

From there, type in Pages in the search, and hit the return key.

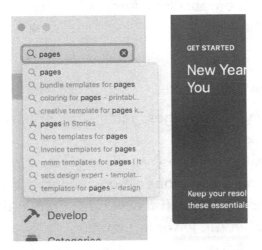

If you have it, the return result will have an Open button; if you don't have it, the result will show a Get button. When you click Get, you'll be prompted to put in your Apple ID and password; if you don't have an Apple ID, then follow the onscreen instructions to get one (this is free).

RUNNING PAGES FOR THE FIRST TIME

When you first open Pages, you'll be asked if you want to use iCloud. I recommend you do; this makes it easy to save and open documents across all devices—if you are writing a document on your phone, for instance, you can open that document and continue working on it from your tablet—it's all very seamless and doesn't require anything extra on your part once it's set up.

If you set up iCloud, you can even access and type documents right in your browser—there's nothing else to install on your computer, which means "technically" you could use Pages on a Windows computer or even a Chromebook or Android device—I'll show you how at the end of this chapter.

THE PAGES CRASH COURSE

The first time you use Pages, you'll get a brief tutorial. You can either watch it or skip it.

Each time you open Pages, you'll be greeted with a directory box that asks you if you want to open a document or if you want to create a new one. We'll be working off a new document in this chapter, so click "New Document" in the lower left corner.

The next box you'll see is all the available templates you can use. A template is a premade document that you can add text into. For example, if you want to write a resume, you can use the resume Template, and you would just keep the formatting but type over the text that's there with the text that matches you. Templates are listed under categories.

If you don't want to start with a template, then click on the first option (which says Blank).

First time users of Pages are often a little disappointed the first time they use Pages; if you've Word, then you have ribbons and menus and options everywhere! Pages looks pretty bare next to that.

Don't worry—looks can be deceiving; there are plenty of options when you know how to find them, and I'll show you each of them in this book.

If you feel overwhelmed already because there are options, you can hide that side panel by clicking on the Format button in the upper right corner.

Now that you have a blank screen, let's go over the very basics of Pages.

SELECT

To select a single word, move your mouse over it and click twice.

SELECT PARAGRAPH

To select all words in the paragraph, click three times over any word in the paragraph you want to select.

SELECT ALL

Select All selects everything in your document. It's a very powerful command! It brings up the same options as Select, but any changes you make will be applied to the entire document.

To Select All, use Command + A on your keyboard.

SELECT OPTIONS

Now that you have the text selected, what do you do? If you click with two fingers on your trackpad or mouse, then the options box comes up. We'll go over what these options are as we continue in the book.

CUT, COPY AND PASTE

To copy and paste words (and images, tables and charts) quicker, you can use keyboard shortcuts.

Selecting content and hitting COMMAND + C will copy it.

Selecting content and hitting COMMAND + X will cut it.

And hitting COMMAND + V will copy the content anywhere you want it in the document.

FIND AND REPLACE

Find and Replace is a handy little feature in Pages that allows you to replace your selection with alternatives.

Let's say you just wrote the opening chapter to your first book. But once you are done, you realize you want your character to be a 'her' instead of a 'him,' and you want to replace all of the "he said" with "she said." It can be done in seconds!

Go to edit from your menu bar, and select Find > Find.

From here you can find all the uses of the word you want to find, but you can also click the down arrow on the left side and select Find & Replace. This lets you search for a word (top line) and replace the word once it finds it (bottom line). When you have both the find and replace word added, then you can click Replace & Find.

DEFINE

Pages has a handy little dictionary built in. You can select any word, tap the trackpad twice to bring up the options menu, and tap Look Up to see the definition of any word.

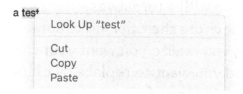

The dictionary will give you multiple definitions (and a thesaurus); even more, you can select options at the bottom to see movies related to the word, Siri Knowledge (which is encyclopedic information), apps related to it, and more!

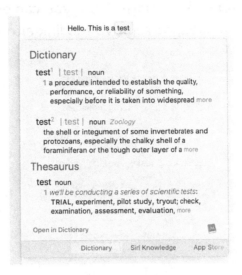

COPY STYLE

The Style command lets you copy and paste styles, like the Microsoft Word format painter feature. If you ever want to make a piece of text look like another, just select the text with the format you'd like to copy, click Format > Copy Style; then select the text you want to alter and click Format > Paste Style. This can be a major time saver!

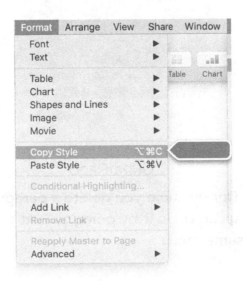

Inserting Hyperlinks

If you want to insert a hyperlink to an internet resource, just type out the link. Pages automatically detects hyperlinks and will insert the link for you. To edit the link or to change the displayed text, just click the link and then tap Link Settings. Here you can edit the link itself, change the text displayed, or remove the link altogether.

. This is a test www.google.com

www.google.com

| Edit | Open Link |

. This is a test www.google.com

Display: www.google.com

Link to: Webpage

Link: www.google.com

| Remove | Open Link |

If you aren't typing a web address, but want to link it to a web address (for example, you are typing: "I go to UCLA" and you want to provide a hyperlink to UCLA), then select the word you want to hyperlink and click with two fingers to bring up the options. From here, just click Add Link and select the kind of link you want to add. You can edit and remove it the same way as in the previous paragraph.

Look Up "test"

Cut
Copy
Paste

Add Link   ▶   Webpage
Speech   ▶   Email
                                 Bookmark

Undo/Redo

If you mess up (for example you delete a paragraph that you shouldn't have) you can Undo it by going to Edit > Undo; you can also redo it under the same menu.

HANDS-ON EXERCISE

This exercise will help you familiarize yourself with the commands we've covered in this section. Just follow the steps below, referring to the above if needed.

Open a blank document.

Type the sentence "The quick brown fox jumps over the lazy dog."

Select the entire sentence.

Copy the sentence.

Tap Enter to start a new line.

Paste the sentence.

In the second sentence, select the word "brown" and replace it with your favorite iPad suggestion.

In the second sentence, add a Phonetics guide to the entire sentence for English learners in the language of your choice (use the guide of your choice). Hint: this sentence can be selected with a triple tap!

Your document should now look like this:

The quick brown fox jumps over the lazy dog.
ザ　クイック　ブロウン　フォックス　ジェンプス　オエル　ザ　ラゼィ　ドグ
The quick grown fox jumps over the lazy dog.

THE FORMATTING TOOLBAR

There are a few menu options to work with in Pages, but in this section, we will be covering the Formatting Toolbar, which is on the right side of your document.

Under Text, it will say "Body" by default. When you click it, you'll see several options. "Body" is normal text in a document—the text you are reading right here would be considered Body Text. Documents have several types of paragraph text; for example, each section of this chapter has a "Heading"—you could just change the font size and make it "look" like a heading, but using a Paragraph Style tells Pages what kind of text it is so it can put together a table of contents later.

Some of the styles will not be very common, "Label Dark" for example.

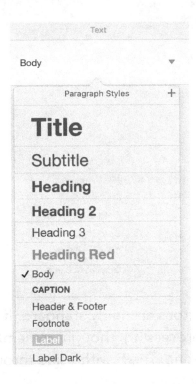

Under this is options for Style, Layout, and More. Let's stay on Style for now, so the next option is Font.

It says 11pt Helvetica; this is the font. If you tap on it, you'll be able to select a new font and adjust the size. Pages offers a healthy font selection, including perennial favorites like Arial, Times New Roman, and Helvetica. Some notable absences include Comic Sans (and yet Papyrus still made the cut), Calibri, and Cambria.

The "regular" dropdown shows you all the style choices for that font (some fonts have different options).

The next three buttons are fairly standard. If you're not familiar with computerized word processing, though, remember B for Bold, I for Italic, and U for underline. The S with a line through it puts a strike across any text you type.

Below this are your alignment buttons. Tap them for options to align your text left, center or right, or justify it. Justified text is text that fills one line exactly. Try it out to see how it works.

The next two buttons are indent buttons. Use them to indent, or to move backwards through indents.

Finally, below this is where you can add bulleted lists and line spacing (if you want to double space, for example).

Hands-On Exercise

This is exercise will help you practice with all of the formatting options available to you in the formatting toolbar.

Type up a heading and a few lines of text in a blank Pages document (you can also use your "quick brown fox" document from the previous exercise if you prefer).

Change your heading so that it appears in Georgia, 20 pt. font, bold, and underlined. Center the heading.

Change the text under the heading so that it is right aligned and italicized.

More Formatting Options in Styles

LAYOUT

The Layout menu lets you put text into columns and adjust line spacing. Yes, you can use Pages to draft that paper for your picky professor who insists on 1.25 spacing (click indents)!

You can also use layout to create columns (if you are writing a newsletter, for example).

MORE

The More option is what you will use for pagination and hyphenation.

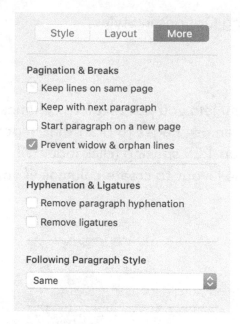

Opening Pages From iCloud

Pages can be run right from your browser; it's great for editing, but for intensive design work, the best solution will be your computer.

To access it from your browser, head to iCloud.com and sign in with your Apple ID.

The first screen you'll see will show you all the things you can do from the cloud; one of them is using Pages. Click it once to open it.

As long as you've been saving your work to the cloud, then any recent docs will show up here, and you can click on their thumbnail once to open them.

You can additionally start a new Doc by clicking on the + button in the upper right corner. This will open up Pages for iCloud. All the features covered in this book can be found in Pages for iCloud as well.

MANAGING DOCUMENTS

Saving in Pages is pretty straightforward—especially if you've used Windows before. It's under File > Save.

Before we move forward with using other features in Pages, I want to go over the less straightforward ways to manage documents.

RENAMING DOCUMENTS

Renaming documents is very easy. Like with many things in Pages, there's more than one way to do it.

The easiest way is when your document is open; just click on the name in the top center of the document.

The next way is File > Rename.

The third way is to find it in Finder, click with two fingers, and select Rename.

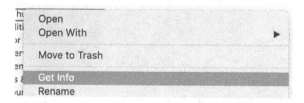

HANDS-ON EXERCISE

These exercises are going to get progressively more challenging! Ready to try your hand at some serious formatting?

Open up a blank Pages document.

Copy and paste a chunk of text from somewhere else (I used the Lorem Ipsum generator at lipsum.org to get five paragraphs of filler text).

Hint: you can visit a webpage and copy text the same way you would in Pages. Then, go back to Pages and paste.

Format it so that it displays as 14 pt., justified, bold, double-spaced red Arial.

Format your text so that it is displayed in three columns. (Remember Columns is under layout.)

Lorem ipsum dolor sit amet, consectetur adipiscing elit. Sed at vestibulum erat. Donec nisi metus, dignissim sed hendrerit ut, congue quis nibh. Nulla nec elit leo. in tempus imperdiet urna nec facilisis. Duis vitae libero a urna feugiat egestas sit amet eu sem. Vestibulum gravida aliquam tortor, ut porta augue varius sed. Maecenas ac massa Fusce sit amet placerat magna. Pellentesque tempor euismod metus quis varius. Sed et odio nec lectus bibendum molestie. Sed vehicula libero eget quam interdum

INSERTING AN IMAGE

Inserting an image can be done several ways. You can copy and paste an image into the document, you can drag a photo into the document, or you can pick it manually.

To pick it manually, you can go to Insert > Choose, and then find the file location.

The quicker way to add a photo, however, is from the menu. Click the image button, which shows you all the different media types you can add. Why would it show movies and music? You can't exactly print those out, right? It shows these options because Pages lets you create interactive electronic documents. This section will focus on photos, however. You can get photos by clicking on Photos or Image Gallery (if the photos are in your gallery) or by clicking "Choose" to pick where the photo is located.

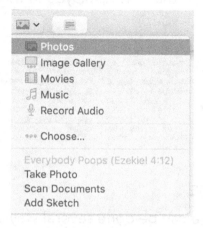

If you pick photos, it's not going to show you all of your photos—just the photos in that photos area of your Mac. You could, for example, have a photo on your USB drive. If that's the case, then you'd want to pick "Choose" from the previous menu instead of photos.

ARRANGING IMAGES

RESIZE AND ROTATE

Once your image is inserted, you can use your mouse to move it, resize it, and rotate it. Resizing is pretty straightforward. Click the image, then move to the corner or side of the image and move the little squares on the edges in and out. To rotate the image you'll do the same thing, but when you get to the corner of the image, press the Command key on your keyboard. This will show you a curved line and also show you the percentage of the rotation as you move the image.

Hint: Looking for images? I often use a website named pexels.com to find public domain (or free to use images).

There's one more way to rotate an image. When you click on the image, you'll notice that the side panel that you used to format text has changed. It's now a new menu with controls to format an image.

There are three buttons on top of this menu (Style, Image, Arrange); we'll go over the first button in the next section, but for this section, go to Arrange.

On the bottom of this menu, there's a section called Rotate; angle is what you want to use. The mouse is a quick and easy way to rotate your image, but if you want precision, then this is the best method. Next to the Angle button, you can also vertically and horizontally flip the image using the arrows.

TEXT WRAP AND PLACEMENT

Let's go back up to the top of the image arrange menu; the first thing you see is Object Placement. The default is Move with Text; this means as you add text above the image, the image moves down. Stay on page means you want it locked into place on the page and it won't move—this is commonly used for watermarks.

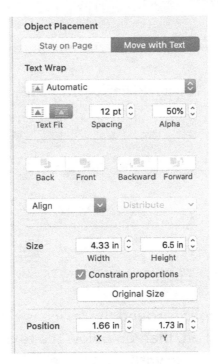

Below this is the Text Wrap. Automatic is the default setting, but if you click on it, you'll notice several other options.

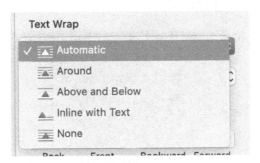

The default option has text above or below the object.

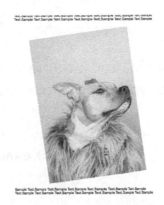

If you want text to wrap around the image, then just click Around.

Notice the white space around the image is kind of tight? If you want it more squared off, then go below the text wrap to Text Fit and you can make it more even with the toggle.

The example below uses the first option under fit.

The next set of options let you pick the size of the image; again, you can do this manually with your mouse, but this lets you be a little more precise.

Finally, the last option lets you pick the placement of the image—if you want it in the middle of the page, for example.

Earlier, I said you could make an image a watermark; great! But you'll notice the options that let you move the image back / forward are greyed out. So how do you make a watermark if you can't move the object behind the text?

It's tricky. The current mode we are using is Word Processing mode. It's much easier to edit and get everything to align right, but options like these will be missing. To make a watermark, we need it to be in Page Layout mode. We can convert it, but we'll lose all of our text, unfortunately.

To convert it, go to File > Convert to Page Layout.

The image can now be moved to the back, but here's the big drawback. Text is now in a text box (see below). That makes dealing with margins and new pages a lot harder. This mode is great for things like fliers; not so good for lengthy documents. So you're out of luck? Not exactly. I'll show you how to add watermarks in a better way later in this chapter.

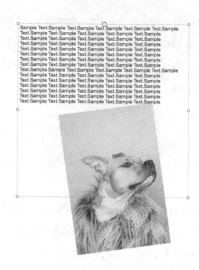

IMAGE GROUPING

There's one last section that's greyed out. Grouping. Grouping is greyed out because you need two images to use it.

Add a second image, then click the image, press command on your keyboard and select the second image; the Group option is no longer greyed out. What grouping does is put two images together, so that when you edit the size, rotation, etc., you are treating the two photos as one image.

If you want to edit just one image, you don't have to ungroup it. You can double click the image to tell Pages that you want to keep them grouped, but you want to make changes to one photo while they are grouped.

WATERMARKS

Earlier, we saw how you couldn't send an object to the background to create a watermark without converting it to Page Layout mode. So that means a word processing document can't have a watermark, right? Nope!

You can create a watermark with something called Section Masters. Once you make all the changes you want to the image and have it where you want it to go, go to Arrange > Section Masters > Move Object to Section Master. It's now a watermark and every new page will show the image.

Edit Mask and Alpha

With your image selected (note: if the images are grouped, you need to double click the image you want to edit—you can't edit both images at the same time), select the Image button.

This brings up options for image enhancements. At the bottom is the Adjustments section; this section is pretty self-explanatory - the Exposure and Saturation sliders will change the amount of exposure / saturation in the image. The Enhance button will do an auto enhancement based on what the computer thinks the image should look like (the reset button will undo it).

Next to the Enhance button is a control button; this will bring up more adjustment controls.

Most people probably won't need this many controls, but it's helpful to know it's there.

The section that may not be as easy to understand is the top section: Edit Mask and Instant Alpha.

Edit Mask is essentially an image crop. You can use this to cut off parts of the image without resizing it.

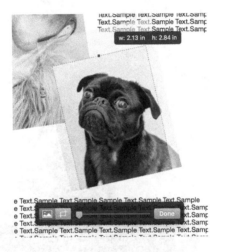

Instant Alpha is one of my personal favorite image editing tools. It removes the background of the image. It's great when your image has a very solid background (you're standing against a solid color wall, for example).

One you click on it, the cursor turns to a square box and you click and drag over the areas you want to take out.

As you click, the sections that are removed will turn a different color to indicate what has been removed. When you're done, let go of the mouse and click the done button.

As you remove the background, it is also autocropping; so if you've removed the background from the top, the image has automatically been cropped to accommodate for it.

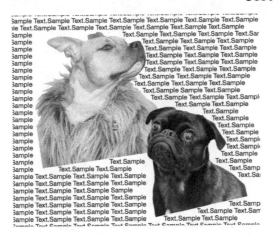

Styling Your Image

Now that we know how to move an image around, let's add some style to it.

To style your image, tap the image. Style is the first button on the image edit menu.

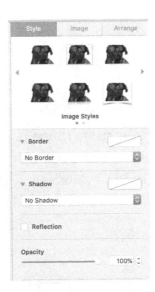

Basic Styles

The top box lets you add quick, pre-defined image styles to your image. For example, if you want your image to have a box around it.

Image Styles

Most people will probably want to do manual editing to the photo, but if you use the arrow in this section, you'll notice a + button. Once you manually make changes to the image (add your transparency, borders, etc.), you can use this button to save these changes, so you can apply them to another photo that you want to have a similar look and feel.

Image Styles

BORDER

The next section is the Border; there is no border on the image by default. If you click the box with the red diagonal line, it will show a drop down of all the different styles available.

Once you pick your border style, you be able to adjust the weight of the border using the slider.

If you click the preview of the border, you will also see all the different border styles for the style that you have picked. Styles vary depending on the style you are using.

SHADOW

Shadows can add a little more dimension to your photo and help it pop off the page more. It works very similar to Borders; click the thumbnail with the red line through it, then pick the shadow style.

Once you pick the style, you'll get several shadow options to increase or decrease the amount of shadowing used.

As you make changes, the image will change in real-time, so you immediately see the effects. Notice in the image below how the image has a more 3D look?

REFLECTION

Reflection is a simple check / uncheck box; you can use the slider to adjust the amount of reflection used, but that's the only edit available.

You can see in the example below how the reflection gave the image the appearance of an image reflecting on the page (the reflection is the darker area on the bottom of the image).

TRANSPARENCY

The final style change is transparency. Transparency makes an image more see-through (see the example below). This is great for something like a watermark, but doesn't help a lot if you don't have something below the image.

In the below example, I put the transparent image above another photo to illustrate how you can use it on top of another image.

HANDS-ON EXERCISE

1. Insert an image into a blank document (or copy and paste the image from the Internet using Command C and Command V).
2. Give the image a special Photo Corners border (or a border of your choosing).
3. Give the image a large, fuzzy shadow.
4. Give the image a 76% reflection.
5. Set the image opacity to 68%.
6. Resize the image so that you can see the full image and its reflection without scrolling.

Your screen should now look something like this:

INSERTING A TABLE

If you have ever added a table in Word, then you may be used to picking the size and width before adding the table; in Pages, you add the table and then adjust it accordingly.

To add a table, tap the Table button from the top menu bar (you can also use Insert > Table from the menu options at the top of MacOS). You'll have several styles to pick from, but again, this is different from Word where you drag to the number of rows and columns that you want.

ADDING COLUMNS AND ROWS

Your table is now inserted, but chances are it's not the right size.

At the bottom of the last row (or the side of the last column) there's a circle with two lines. Click on either of those to adjust the number of columns / rows. You can either use the up / down arrows to pick, or you can click the number and then type the amount you want.

INTERACTING WITH TABLES

It can be a little tricky to work with a table in Pages at first. Double clicking a cell will bring up the keyboard, but single clicking it will select the entire cell (Microsoft Excel users should have an easier time with this concept).

If there's no text, you can single click and start typing, but if you want to edit the text that's already there, then you need to double click.

ROW / COLUMN OPTIONS

If you want to delete or add a row / column, then go to the row or column you want to make changes to, and then click the drop-down arrow. Several options will come up.

You can also click the number associated with the row / column to select all. This is helpful if you want to copy / paste a row or column.

STYLING TABLES

Apple's predefined tables look great, but if you've got a specific color scheme or style in mind, it's easy to customize your tables to match that. Just select your table (or certain cells in your table) and look to the right side menu, which has changed to a table style menu.

TABLE OPTIONS

The first set of options are for the entire table.

These are all options that would change everything in the table. Such as the table outline; if you can see grids and alternating row colors (if you want row 1 white, row 2 black, row 3 white, row 4 black, etc.). You can also increase the font size and add new rows and columns.

The Table Styles at the top are similar to the image styles; they're predefined styles.

CELL OPTIONS

The table options are great if you want to change everything about the table. But what if you just want to change a cell, column, or row? That's where the Cell Option tab comes into play.

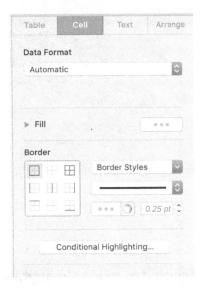

It says "Cell" but Cell here is anything that you highlight. So if you highlight one cell, then it's just that cell; but if you highlight multiple cells, then it's each of those cells.

Data Format is where you can change what is inside the cell; what does that mean? Let's say one of your columns had only currency; you could highlight that column and then say that everything in those cells were currency; so a dollar sign would be added to all the numbers in the cells.

You can change the color of the cell under Fill; you can change the border style, border color, and border weight under Border.

Conditional Highlighting is a little less obvious than those first couple of options.

This lets you create rules; for example anytime you have a cell with the number 2, the cell text turns Bold.

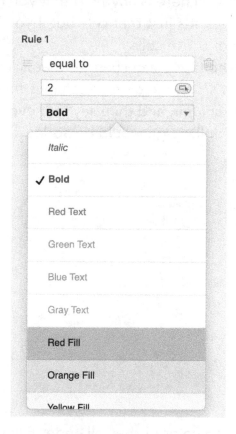

TEXT OPTIONS

By now you should understand how to format text. It's no different when you are doing a table. The same rules as before apply—any cell you highlight will have the text changed—so if you have the entire row highlighted, then all the text in those cells changes.

There is one box worth noting: Wrap text in cell. It's just a check / uncheck box, but it's important because if you have a long string of text and you want it to fit within a cell without going into the next cell, then you need it to wrap.

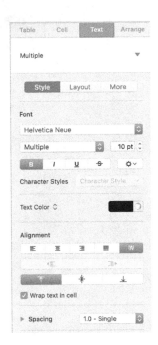

Here's an example of wrapping off.

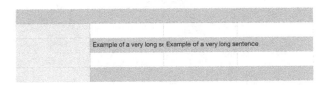

And here's what it looks like on.

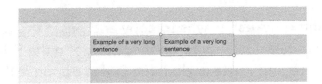

ARRANGE OPTIONS

Just like text options are the same as formatting options outside of the table, Arrange Options are almost identical to the options covered in Photo Arrangement options.

DELETING TABLES

Deleting an entire table is a quick process. Click the table. Hit delete.

IMPORTING TABLES

Importing a table from somewhere else can be done a few different ways.

The first, and quickest, way is to copy and paste the table. Command V is obviously the easiest way to do this, but go to the Edit menu. Notice there are a Paste and Paste and Match Styles options? If you aren't getting the paste results that you want, try this Paste instead.

Edit	Insert	Format	Arrange	View
Undo Wrap Text in Cell Setting				⌘Z
Redo Typing				⇧⌘Z
Cut				⌘X
Copy				⌘C
Paste				⌘V
Paste and Match Style				⌥⇧⌘V

If you don't need to make changes to the table, what a lot of people prefer to do is just make a screenshot of the spreadsheet: Command + Shift + 3 (or Command + Shift + 4 if you want to do only select areas of the screen).

HANDS-ON EXERCISE

This one's a little more of a challenge!

1. Insert a table with the style of your choice.
2. Adjust the table so that it contains three rows and three columns (including headers)
3. Enter labels for each row and column and numerical data in each cell.
4. Select your bottom row and copy it.
5. Add an additional row.
6. Paste your copied row into the new row.
7. Select the whole table and turn alternating rows on.
8. Turn on Header Row Lines.
9. Change the Table Font to Arial.
10. Select your column headers. Change them to a green fill with blue bold underlined text centered in the middle of the cell and right aligned.

Now your screen should look something like this:

	Column 1	Column 2
Row 1	1	2
Row 2	3	4
Row 2	3	4

INSERTING A CHART

To insert a chart in Pages, tap the Insert button, then tap Charts. From here, you'll choose the type of chart (bar, area, line, pie), as well as the style you want. Choose from several different color schemes in 2D, 3D, and interactive. If you change your mind about your chart choice, you can always change it later, without losing any data you've entered. Just tap on your favorite chart to insert it into your document.

As with almost everything in Pages, you can also add Charts from the top menu (Insert > Chart).

Once you have your chart picked, a chart that's already filled out will be added to your document (I'm using a Pie chart in this chapter, but the same features apply to almost all of the charts—they just look a little different).

EDITING CHART DATA

It's so nice for Pages to put a pretty chart that's all filled out into our document, right? Sure! But wouldn't it be nicer if it had meaningful data? To add your own data, click Edit Chart Data. This brings up a mini table that you can edit with whatever information you want.

I'm going to replace the months with the names of states, and use an entirely different data range. The chart changes with each change I make in the table. Notice that the chart below is completely different from the one above?

You can enter additional rows if you need to—but this won't work on all charts (like the pie chart).

STYLING YOUR PIE CHART

Now that you have the data you want, it's time to style it.

If you did a pie chart, then you'll see three options on the side (Chart, Wedges, Arrange).

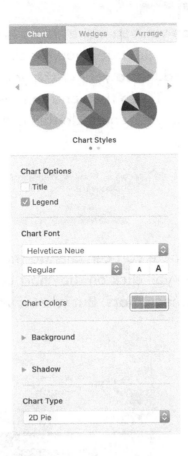

Other charts (like bar charts) have four (Chart, Axis, Series, Arrange).

I'll go over the two extra options for a bar chart in the next section.

In the Chart section you can make changes to the entire chart. By default the chart has no title, but if you check off the box, a title (cleverly named "Title") is added to your chart; you'll probably want to name it something else. To do that (and this also applies to renaming pretty much anything in your chart) double click on it and start typing.

Below the title is where you can change the font, and under that, the chart colors. When you click on the chart colors, it gives you a whole host of pre-defined colors. But what if you want to pick your own?

There's one extra small step to picking your own colors. You have to double click on the wedge that you want to change the color of, and then over on the menu options to the right of it, click Style (Style is a new option that's only there if you double click the wedge). From here, you can pick a color under "Fill."

While we are in this section, let's go just under it to Stroke and Shadow. Both of these options help a wedge stand out a little. This is useful if you want to illustrate one area of the chart over others. See in the example below how I added a dotted line (and increased the line weight to 4) and also added a shadow.

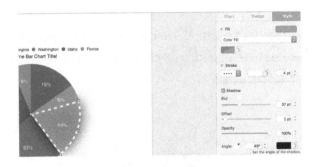

If you really want that wedge to stand out, try pulling it apart from the chart. You can do that by clicking on the Wedge option, and then changing the Wedge Position. Look at the example below; the wedge is now separated in the chart.

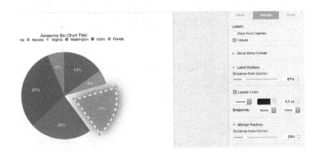

Now let's go back to the chart section and look at the other options we can apply to the entire chart. You can give it a background, add a shadow to it, and finally, change the Chart Type. You can make it a different Pie chart or turn it into a line chart (note: this will probably interfere with your data and you may have to redo some of it).

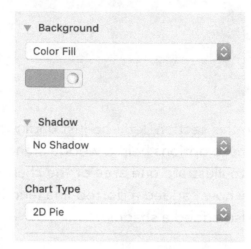

We saw how going to the Wedge section could separate your single wedge from the rest. If you don't double click the wedge and change it, below is what happens.

All the wedges separate. If that's what you want, then perfect! If that's not what you want, undo and then double click the wedge you want to separate.

Checking off Data Point Names will put the names of the value in chart (you can also keep it in the Legend).

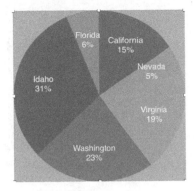

The values on the chart are currently shown as percentages; if you prefer showing them as numbers (or another value type), you can change this under Value Format.

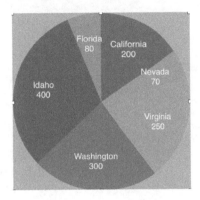

If you check off Lender Lines, you probably won't notice a difference; to see what the lines are, click the Straight drop-down and change it to Angled.

You should now see lines to the sides of the chart.

The arrange option should look familiar to you. You've seen it in the Tables section and the Photos section; it's the same features.

STYLING YOUR BAR CHART

Now that you know how to style a Pie Chart, you'll have no problem with the Bar Chart; it's basically the same, but with more options for labels.

In the axis sub-tab, you can turn category labels, series names, gridlines, and titles on and off. Similarly, in the Y-axis or X-axis sub-tab, you can turn value labels, gridlines, and titles on and off. Here you can also specify the number format you'd like to use and adjust the value scale settings. Number formatting includes the option to add prefixes and suffixes, like currency symbols or suffixes like %, millions, etc.

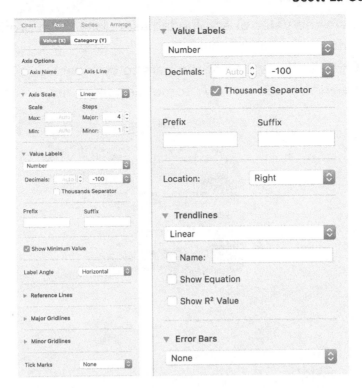

Note: the contents of the sub-tabs change depending on the orientation of your chart. The number formatting option may appear under either the x- or y-axis, depending on the type of chart you've inserted.

HANDS-ON EXERCISE

Let's create a chart! Create a chart with the following specifications:

1. Insert a 3D bar chart.
2. Edit the data so that it shows how much money Company A and Company B made in the years 2010, 2011, and 2012 (amounts are up to you!).
3. Show gridlines on the chart for both the x and y-axis.
4. Give the chart the title "Profits of Company A and Company B."
5. Give the category axis the title "Year" and the value axis the title "Profits."
6. Remember that the x and y axes depend on what orientation your bar chart is in.

7. Give the value axis value labels a dollar sign prefix and a K suffix.

8. Change the shape of the bars to cylinders.

Your screen should now look something like this:

INSERTING A SHAPE

To insert a shape into a document, click the shape button or go to Insert > Shape from the top menu. This will bring up all the shapes available for you. Find the one you like and click it to insert it.

Remember that you can change the color, border and shadow/reflection effects later!

Shapes sounds a little misleading. If you're like me, you're probably thinking square, circle, etc. But shapes in Pages are kind of like clipart. Yes, basic shapes are there, but so are other things. In the example below I searched for "Dog" and got five results!

RESIZING SHAPES AND ADJUSTING PROPORTIONS

Shape resizing is just like resizing photos: tap on a corner and drag it to the desired size. However, with Shapes, you can also adjust proportions. What does that mean? It's better shown than explained. Double tap your trackpad on the shape to bring up the shape options. Now click "Make Editable."

There's now a bunch of dots on the shape. These represent points that you can adjust.

As an example, I moved the point inward from the dog's stomach and look what happened.

By default you make these changes with a curved point, but you can change this by bringing the options up again. Notice the three different points?

MOVING AND ROTATING SHAPES

To move a shape, simply tap on it and drag it to a new location. To rotate a shape, click the image then press the command button—just like you would an image.

ADDING TEXT TO A SHAPE

To add text on top of a shape, double-tap on it to activate its text field. Then just type your text!

CREATING TEXT BOXES

There's one more type of shape, but it's not under shape. It's a Text Box. Text Boxes are exactly what they sound like—floating boxes that have text.

Why use a Text Box instead of typing out the text? Ideally, you want to use them when you are making something like a title—not when you are typing out your epic novel. It's for short text that you want to stand out.

Unlike standard text, Text Boxes are treated in the same way images are, so you can easily move them around and have other things wrap around them.

To get started, click the T in the menu.

You can also do Insert > Text Box.

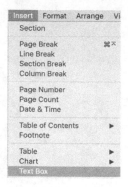

This puts a floating box with generic text in your document.

You can change the color of the box and more by clicking on Style; it has all the same types of options that you'd find in the Image or Shape options.

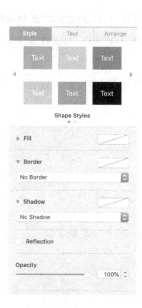

Because it's a Shape, you are able to edit it like you would a shape. In the below example, I curved out the bottom portion of the box.

STYLING SHAPES AND TEXT BOXES

Styling Shapes and Text boxes is the same as styling an image, so I won't repeat myself here. If you are confused about styling, referred to the section in the Photos chapter.

HANDS-ON EXERCISE

Let's practice using shapes and text boxes. Follow the directions below.

1. Insert two shapes of your choice.
2. Make one shape blue with a gradient and texture. Give it a solid 1 px black border. Add a shadow effect and reduce its opacity to 50%.
3. Make the other shape red with a gradient. Add a shadow effect.
4. Add text to each shape – make one read "Blue" and the other "Red."
5. Make the text white, underlined, and in Marker Felt typeface. Hint: don't forget about copying and pasting styles!

Now your screen should look something like this.

ENTERING DOCUMENT SETUP MODE

To use Document Setup, you can go to View > Inspector > Document Setup.

You can also use the Format / Document toggle icons in the menu bar to switch between them.

This brings up your main document editor with three tab options: Document, Section, Bookmarks.

CHANGING DOCUMENT MARGINS AND SIZE

In Document Setup, the settings that pertain to margins and paper size are all found in the first tab: Document.

At the top of the settings, under Printer and Paper Size, you can see all the different paper sizes available. Keep in mind that changing to a different printer may give you more (or less) sizes.

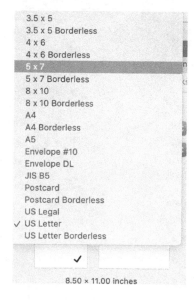

Below this, you can change the orientation of the paper from portrait to landscape.

Finally, you can change the margins under Document Margins. One inch all around is the default setting.

To change the margins, go to Document Setup, then drag the margins to where you would like them to go. Tap "Done" when you are finished.

CREATING CUSTOM PAPER SIZE

What about if you don't see your size? You can create a custom size, but keep in mind if you are printing the document, it may not print correctly.

To create a custom size, go to File > Page Setup.

Next, click the drop down under Paper Size.

Finally, add your custom size.

HYPHENATIONS AND LIGATURES

At the bottoms of Document Setup are two checkboxes: Hyphenations and Ligatures. Checking them turns them on and off.

Hyphenation puts a dash next to long words at the end of the page margin—the idea is to make the document look more even by breaking up a word and continuing it on the next line.

le text. This is sample
is sample text. This is
t. This is sample text.
iple text. This is sam-
is sample text. This is
t. This is sample text.

Ligatures are two letters that are combined together to create one character. See some examples below.

$$AE \rightarrow \text{Æ}$$
$$ae \rightarrow \text{æ}$$
$$OE \rightarrow \text{Œ}$$
$$oe \rightarrow \text{œ}$$
$$ff \rightarrow \text{ff}$$
$$fi \rightarrow \text{fi}$$

HEADERS AND PAGE NUMBERS

One of the most useful features of Document Setup Mode is its header and footer options. These document elements will appear on every page of your document. You'll also be able to add page numbers from here.

You can control the size of the Header / Footer in the Document section of Setup.

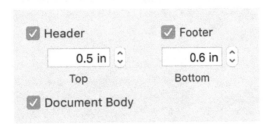

The placement of the Header / Footer is controlled in Section.

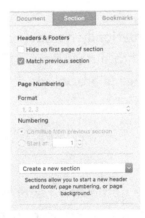

Section lets you tell Pages not to put your Header / Footer on your title page, for example, or to have your numbering start at a certain page.

To insert your Header / Footer, just move your cursor to the top of the page; you'll see a table of sorts with three cells—these represent left, right and center align. You'll also have the option to add the page number to any of these cells.

BOOKMARKS

Bookmarks are perfect for electronic works. When you add a bookmark it indexes it, and then you can later hyperlink to that bookmark. So you could be on page 2 of a 500 page document, and have it reference a bookmark on page 87; when the user clicks it, it jumps to the section bookmarked.

To create one, highlight the text you want to bookmark, go to the Bookmark tab of Document Setup, and click the Add Bookmark button.

The bookmark is automatically named whatever text you highlighted. So if the text you highlighted says "This is a bookmark" then the bookmark is called "This is a bookmark".

You can single click the name and rename it. This will only change the name of the bookmark and not the text itself.

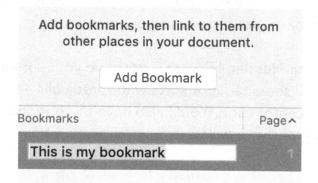

TABLE OF CONTENTS

If you are working with a document that needs a table of contents, then you first need to make sure you are using the correct headings. Headings tell Pages what will go into the table of contents.

To create a heading, highlight the text you want to be the heading (a chapter title, for example), then go to the format side bar.

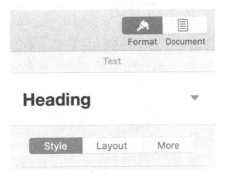

Click the drop down next to Heading and select the type of heading. Heading is usually chapter titles; heading 2 is usually sections; and heading 3 is sections within sections.

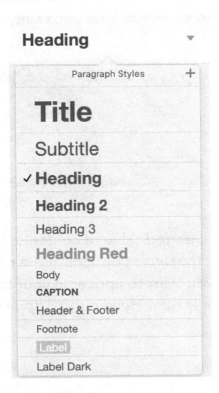

Clicking the arrow next to the heading lets you change how it's formatted; for example, if you want your heading to match the formatting you have, then just click Redefine from Selection.

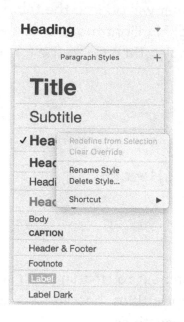

Once you have all the headings in the document, then go to Insert > Table of Contents and select the kind you want. Document is the most common.

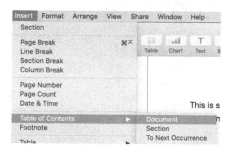

If you click on the inserted table of contents, there will be a table of contents formatter in the format options in the right pane of Pages; you can select what you want to appear in your table of contents here. For example, if you only want Heading 1 to appear, then uncheck everything else.

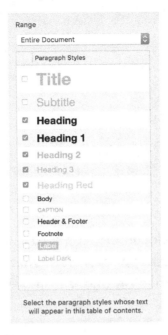

Insert Footnotes

To insert a footnote into your document, highlight the text you want to add a footnote to, then select Insert > Footnote.

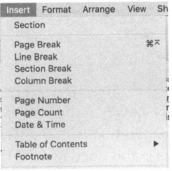

Insert Comment

If you are editing someone's document and want to add a comment, highlight the sentence you want to add a comment to, right click (or click with two fingers) and add your comment, then click done.

TRACK CHANGES

If you are editing a document, it's also a good idea to turn on Track Changes; this lets the other person see what you have changed.

Track changes is turned on under Edit > Track Changes (it's turned off in the same place).

When it's turned on, a new bar appears at the top of the document, and the color of the changed text is also different. The user now has to accept or reject changes in the document; if they reject them, then the changes go away.

Syncing Documents with iCloud

If you've enabled iCloud in your Pages app, your documents will be synced across your devices automatically, with absolutely no work required on your part. You can even access your documents online from any internet connection at www.icloud.com.

Emailing a Document From Pages

E-mailing documents is one of the most straightforward methods of sharing your document. Go to Share > Send a Copy.

Collaborating

You can also collaborate on a document by going to Share > Collaborate With Others.

This brings up an option that asks how you would like the share the document.

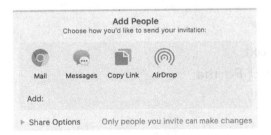

I recommend clicking on the Share Options drop down to make sure the right permissions are enabled. For example, you can make the document readable to anyone you share it with or anyone who gets the document; you can also give the user permission to make changes.

EXPORT A PAGES DOCUMENT

By default, you'll be saving your file as a .Pages document. That's great if you have Pages, but if you're sharing it with (or opening it on) a computer that doesn't have pages, or you want to create a universal PDF that anyone can see, then you'll need to export it.

This is pretty straightforward. Go to File > Export.

There are six different file types:
- PDF
- Word
- EPUB
- Plain Text
- Rich Text Format
- Pages '09

PDF is the best option if you want to preserve all the formatting in the document and make it look exactly as it appears in Pages. Plain Text will take out all the formatting but be readable on pretty much any editor. ePub is what you would use if you want to create an eBook of your document that can be opened on something like iBooks. Some eReaders don't open ePubs natively and will convert them—so formatting might not be retained.

PRINTING

To print a document, go to File > Print.

At the bottom of the print menu, there's also an option to save as a PDF. It's Pages' version of Print to File.

APPENDIX: KEYBOARD SHORTCUTS

GENERAL SHORTCUTS

Command-X – Cuts or removes selected text or item and copies it to the clipboard.

Command-C – Copies the selected text or item to the clipboard.

Command-V – Pastes the contents of the clipboard into the document, app, or Finder.

Command-Z – Undoes the previous command.

Command- Shift-Z – Redoes the previous undo.

Command-A – Selects all text or items in the running program.

Command-F – Opens the Find window to find documents or other items.

Command-G – Finds the next occurrence of a previously found item (i.e. Find Again).

Command-H – Hides the current running program or front window (Note: this will not work if you have a program running in full screen).

Command-Option-H – Hides all the open apps and windows.

Command-M – Minimizes the currently open window or app (Note: this will not work if you have a program running in full screen).

Command-Option-M – Minimizes all open apps and windows.

Command-N – Opens a new document or window.

Command-O – Opens an item (for instance if you are in Word or Pages and you want to open a previously saved document).

Command-P – Prints the current website or document.

Command-S – Saves the current document.

Command-W – Closes the front window or app

Command-Option-W – Closes all open apps and windows.

Command-Q – Quits an app.

Command-Option-Esc – Force quits a program that is not responding.

Command-Space Bar – Brings up Spotlight to quickly find documents, emails, and apps.

Command-Tab – Switches to the next open app (Note: if you don't let go of Command and continue hitting the Tab button, you can continue going to the next app).

Command-Shift-3 – Takes a screenshot of your entire screen.

Command-, – Opens the Preference menu (if applicable) for the current app.

DOCUMENT SHORTCUTS

The following shortcuts are applicable to supported document software like Word, PowerPoint, Pages, Excel, OpenOffice, etc.

Command-B – Bold or un-bold the selected text.

Command-I – Italicize or un-italicize selected text.

Command-U – Underline or remove underline to selected text.

ABOUT THE AUTHOR

Scott La Counte is a librarian and writer. His first book, *Quiet, Please: Dispatches from a Public Librarian* (Da Capo 2008) was the editor's choice for the Chicago Tribune and a Discovery title for the Los Angeles Times; in 2011, he published the YA book The N00b Warriors, which became a #1 Amazon bestseller; his most recent book is *#OrganicJesus: Finding Your Way to an Unprocessed, GMO-Free Christianity* (Kregel 2016). His latest book is *Jesus Ascended. What Does That Mean?*

He has written dozens of best-selling how-to guides on tech products.

You can connect with him at ScottDouglas.org.

CPSIA information can be obtained
at www.ICGtesting.com
Printed in the USA
BVHW010345040620
580898BV00007B/398